# GOLF IN WALES
## A PICTORIAL HISTORY

PHIL *&* TRUDY CARRADICE

AMBERLEY

# THE AUTHORS

PHIL CARRADICE is a full-time writer and broadcaster. He has written over forty books, from novels and poetry to history and biography. He recently published *Nautical Training Ships* with Amberley and is currently researching a pictorial history of the First World War. He regularly broadcasts on Radio 4 and presents the BBC Wales History programme *The Past Master*.

TRUDY CARRADICE is a former editor of *The South Wales Golfer*. She represented Wales in the Women's Senior Home International matches on two occasions and has been club champion in three separate golf clubs. Her love of golf has taken her to courses all over the world and has provided the inspiration for this publication. A long-time collector of golf memorabilia, this is her first book.

First published 2010

Amberley Publishing Plc
Cirencester Road, Chalford,
Stroud, Gloucestershire, GL6 8PE
www.amberley-books.com

Copyright © Phil & Trudy Carradice, 2010

The right of Phil & Trudy Carradice to be identified as the Authors of this work has been asserted in accordance with the Copyrights, Designs and Patents Act 1988.

ISBN 978 1 84868 836 0

British Library Cataloguing in Publication Data.
A catalogue record for this book is available from the British Library.

Typeset in 9.5pt on 12pt Celeste.
Typesetting by Amberley Publishing.
Printed in the UK.

# CONTENTS

# ACKNOWLEDGEMENTS

Thanks are due to the directors, secretaries and executive officers of the various clubs and unions contacted whilst compiling this book.

Particular thanks must be given to the following individuals:

Paul Williams, who contributed the editorial piece on the Celtic Manor
Richard Dixon and Liz Edwards of the Golf Union of Wales
Russell Thomas and Paul Mayo of Newport Golf Club
Alan Hughes of Southerndown Golf Club
Beverly Cronin of Pyle & Kenfig Golf Club
Barney Curnock of Morlais Castle Golf Club
Simon Edwards of Builth Wells Golf Club
Einion Angel of Caernarfon Golf Club
Richard West of Wrexham Golf Club
Ian Chambers of Brecon Golf Club
Claire Sobik of Monmouthshire Golf Club

Apologies to anybody missed from the above list.

Special thanks need to be given to all those golfers and postcard enthusiasts who have helped in compiling the authors' collection.

# INTRODUCTION

The sport of golf has been around for many years. Some people believe it to have been played in China as early as the tenth century. Others say the game originated on the frozen rivers of Holland in the fifteenth century, a combination of ice hockey and what we now call golf. Both Mary, Queen of Scots, and her son James, who later became James I of England and James VI of Scotland, are known to have played the game north of the border in the sixteenth century.

Golf may have been enjoyed by many, but to some, it was no more than a confounded nuisance. Fifty years before Mary and James ever picked up a club, another Scottish king, James II, had been so exasperated by the leisure activities of his subjects that he declared, 'Futebaw and golf be utterly crypt done and not usyt.' What he was doing was expressing his concern that popular enjoyment of both sports was interfering with the archery practice of the Scots, something that was vital for the defence of his realm. James could have saved his breath; football and golf had come to stay.

The game of golf had also long been popular in England, many people believing that English interest in the game actually predates the Scottish involvement. For proof of this, you need look no further than the fourteenth century 'Crecy window' in Gloucester Cathedral. It seemingly depicts a character swinging a golf club, thereby indicating that golf has a long heritage in England as well as Scotland.

Golf in Wales, however, seems to be much more modern in origin, for it was not until the nineteenth century that the sport become fashionable in the Principality. Unlike rugby, the game was not deeply embedded in the Welsh psyche. Most people were too busy earning a living, either on the land or down the mines, to even consider spending time creating and playing on golf courses. The upper classes, the squires, landowners and coal magnates of the country, might well have played golf, but they did so when holidaying in England or north of the border.

However, in sport, as in so much of our social history, the Victorian Age brought change. The Welsh hierarchy wanted their own courses, and by January 1895, representatives of seven Welsh golf clubs attended a meeting in Shrewsbury in order to form the Welsh

The Crecy Window, dating from the middle of the fourteenth century, in Gloucester Cathedral.

Golfing Union. It was a seminal moment. Even so, golf in Wales, as in the rest of Britain, remained largely a sport for the upper classes for the next hundred years, until the final decades of the twentieth century, in fact, when there was an explosion of interest and the creation of dozens of new courses.

What Wales may have lacked in longevity, it has more than made up for in the quality and atmosphere of its courses. Tenby, arguably the oldest club in Wales, remains a stunningly beautiful layout, as do the other great links of the country, places like Royal St David's at Harlech, Aberdovey, Borth and Ynyslas, Ashburnham and Royal Porthcawl. Wales also boasts a plethora of what can be justifiably called 'hidden gems'. Courses like Dolgellau, the two Newports – in Pembrokeshire and Gwent – Llandrindod Wells, Whitchurch and Radyr offer the golfer an experience and a welcome that are unique to Wales.

This book does not purport to be a full and detailed account of every single course in Wales. Such an undertaking would undoubtedly be informative and instructive but, as far as most people who enjoy playing golf are concerned, would hardly be particularly interesting. This is a very personal selection of courses that we have played and enjoyed over the years. If readers disagree, if readers have their own favourite courses, then that is fine. That merely

*Above:* The popularity of golf!

*Right:* Dai Rees, arguably Wales' greatest ever golfer.

extends and continues the debate about what we firmly believe to be some of the loveliest courses in Britain.

Through this book we hope to whet the appetite of golfers and lay readers alike. The use of old photographs, postcards and ephemera will, we believe, stir an interest in anyone who loves the game of golf and is looking for that little extra edge of enthusiasm. Modern photographs, where used, bring the courses up to date.

Golf in Wales might have a short history but the influence of Welsh golfers and Welsh courses remains strong. Amateur and professional, men and women, the list of Welsh golfers is a renowned one. Most people have heard of Ian Woosnam, but he was only one of three Welshmen to captain the Ryder Cup team. Dai Rees and Brian Huggett preceded him in the role. And it's not just captains. Wales has provided six Ryder Cup players over the years – Woosnam, Rees and Huggett all having played for the team before captaining it. The other three golfers were Bert Hodson – the first Welshman to play Ryder Cup golf, in 1931 – Dave Thomas and Phil Price.

The year 2010 is special for Welsh golf, as in the autumn, the series of Ryder Cup matches between Europe and the USA are due to be held at the Celtic Manor Resort, the first time the competition has been held in Wales. The Ryder Cup, the biannual tournament that has been running since 1927, is the third largest sporting event in the world. And Wales is gearing itself up for an influx of golf enthusiasts and players.

If nothing else, the Ryder Cup will stimulate an interest in Welsh golf and Welsh golf courses. We would hope that this book only further encourages visitors and locals alike to venture out onto the glorious fairways and greens of some of the finest golf courses you will ever discover.

Phil & Trudy Carradice, St Athan, 2010

# THE EARLY YEARS
# 1888 TO 1900

The Welsh Golfing Union, now known as the Golf Union of Wales following the recent merger of the men's and ladies' unions, was founded in 1895 when seven Welsh clubs were invited to a meeting at the Raven Hotel in Shrewsbury. At that stage, twenty clubs were in existence in the Principality, but not all of them were able to send representatives to the meeting. The seven clubs that did attend were Rhyl, Caernarfon, Merionethshire, Aberdovey, Borth & Ynyslas, Glamorganshire, and Porthcawl.

Clubs not able to attend, but claiming an interest, included Tenby, Swansea, St David's (later Royal St David's at Harlech), Ashburnham, Montgomeryshire, and the North Wales Club at Llandudno.

The 1880s and 1890s witnessed a considerable surge of interest in the game of golf, both in Wales and in Britain as a whole. This was due, in many respects, to the growth of the Victorian middle class. For the first time in their lives, people found themselves with the time and the inclination to engage in leisure activities. Many of the earliest courses in Wales were founded because of the holiday boom as men and women travelled westward to enjoy the beauties of the Welsh coastline.

Golf in the final years of the nineteenth century was, therefore, popular, but it remained a middle- and upper-class pursuit. Interestingly, because of the holiday element, women in Wales, residents and visitors alike, were always encouraged to take up the game. Things did not change for some time, even the Artisan courses that were later attached to some clubs being a product of the early twentieth century. The early days of Welsh golf were undoubtedly 'rough and ready', but these first courses and first clubs were laying the foundations of what lay ahead.

There are several courses that lay claim to be the first ever golf club in Wales. These range from Tenby in Pembrokeshire to Borth and Ynyslas in Ceredigion and Pontnewydd on the eastern edge of the Principality. All of the claims are substantial and are taken very seriously by the members of each individual club.

## TENBY GOLF CLUB

It is a fact of history that the mayor of Tenby once adjourned a court early in order to play a game of golf on the dunes outside the town. This was recorded in a book written in 1875, so it is clear that the game of golf was being played at Tenby several years prior to the establishment of the club. Be that as it may, it was in 1888 that the club at Tenby was founded. Pontnewydd Golf Club in Cwmbran also claims early establishment, believing that its course and club were founded thirteen years earlier in 1875. Unfortunately, there are no written records to corroborate this, and so, for the time being at least, the honour of being the first golf club in Wales belongs to Tenby.

The course at Tenby lies on land behind South Beach, stretching out towards Giltar Point opposite Penally village. It is a fine links course that has hosted numerous international and championship events over the years. It began life as a nine-hole course but was reconstructed in 1902 when James Braid came to Tenby to advise on the reconstruction – for a fee of £6.00.

One of the fairways at Porthcawl.

Sand, sand and more sand at Royal St David's, Harlech.

The golf links at Tenby.

Narrow wheeled trolleys on this 1950s view of Tenby Golf Club.

The course was extended to a full eighteen holes in 1907, three of these holes being parkland rather than links and reached by crossing the Tenby to Pembroke railway line. There are many memorable holes here, but the third has one of the most difficult greens you will ever encounter: a wicked sloping surface that runs from back to front. If the pin is at the front of the green, you certainly do not want to be above it, as if you miss the hole, you will be left with a good 20- to 30-yard pitch back on.

In the early days of the club, there was no golf on Sundays. There was considerable debate about this, with opposition from the clergy and letters to the press before the matter was put to a meeting of members. Sunday golf was vetoed by twenty votes to twelve and it was not until 1920 that servicemen returning from the First World War overwhelmingly endorsed Sunday golf at the first postwar General Meeting.

Tenby is a demanding but enjoyable course that forces you to concentrate hard all the way around – something that is often very hard to do when you stand on the dunes above South Beach and gaze out towards the low, flat bulk of Caldey Island. Hit straight, avoid the dunes, and stay out of the bunkers – great advice for playing this wonderful links course.

## PONTNEWYDD GOLF CLUB

Arguably the oldest course in Wales, Pontnewydd Golf Club claims to have been founded in 1875. Although there are no remaining records, local historians from the area insist that golfers regularly came to the course by train, and then by walking or by riding in a horse-driven brake from the local station, in the days before cars were readily available. Members, only partly in jest, often refer to the club as 'Royal Pontnewydd', an accolade it might never have been given but one that the course certainly deserves and enjoys.

Pontnewydd is an eleven-hole mountainside course, golfers playing seven of the holes twice (albeit from different tee positions) in order to complete a full eighteen holes. The original clubhouse was a beautiful wooden pavilion, but this was replaced and a new clubhouse built

The original clubhouse at Pontnewydd.

at the end of the twentieth century. Playing the course can involve a degree of hard walking, but to compensate, there are some magnificent views across the Severn Estuary.

Trees and deep rough line the fairways. Accuracy rather than length is the key to playing well at Pontnewydd. The course is 'quirky', but it has an atmosphere that is immensely appealing, one that will bring visitors back time and time again.

Club members have achieved notable success over the years, winning the Welsh Team Championship on several occasions. Many club members, like Tim Dyke, now plying his trade on the professional circuits, have gone on to become full Welsh internationals – and that speaks volumes about the quality of the course.

## GLAMORGANSHIRE GOLF CLUB

Founded in 1890 and situated in Penarth, still one of the most popular holiday destinations in South Wales, Glamorganshire Golf Club has many claims to fame. To start with, this was where the Stableford system of scoring was first tried out. Invented by Dr Frank Stableford while he was a member of the club, the system was first played at Glamorganshire in 1898, even though Stableford himself then moved on to become a member of Wallasey Golf Club in England, and the scoring system was not officially launched until 1931.

In the early twentieth century, the Barbarian Rugby Club made Glamorganshire their official headquarters, with players enjoying a relaxing game of golf after their matches on their traditional Easter Tour of South Wales. Guy Gibson, leader of the Dam Buster raids, was a member here for a short while, a memorable party being held in the clubhouse when news of his VC came through.

Club member Henry Howell was Welsh amateur champion eight times and, in 1927, took on an amazing bet – to complete the eighteen-hole course in as few shots as possible in an hour and a quarter. He completed his round in sixty-three shots in just 68 minutes. And, of course, he won his bet.

The course and clubhouse of Glamorganshire.

Glamorganshire is a parkland course with huge trees and a couple of steep climbs. Relatively short by modern standards, this is still a great test of skill. And the views out over the Bristol Channel as you stand on the seventeenth tee are spectacular. The clubhouse looks just as it would have done at the turn of the nineteenth century, an atmospheric and enjoyable end to your day's golf.

## ROYAL PORTHCAWL GOLF CLUB

Arguably the most famous course in Wales, Royal Porthcawl has hosted many international events and championships – including the 1995 Walker Cup. Founded in 1891, this is a links course of real character, history, and tradition.

Narrow fairways are guarded by gorse, tough marram grass and, as you would expect on a links course of this standard, deep bunkers. Play Royal Porthcawl on a fine summers day and it seems almost benign. But when the wind and rain hammer in off the Bristol Channel, this can prove to be one of the toughest tests of golf in Britain – as Tiger Woods and his compatriots discovered during their 14-10 defeat in the 1995 Walker Cup.

A links course of just over 6,000 yards, Porthcawl is not long by modern standards yet the sea is ever-present and the Bristol Channel is in sight from every single hole. You can see it, smell it, sometimes even feel it when the waves crash in fury onto the rocks of Sker Point below you. With the first three holes closely bordering the coastline, any hooked ball runs the real danger of finishing up on the beach or in the water. The eighteenth – a downhill par four into the prevailing wind – is one of the finest finishing holes in Wales. It is difficult to hold a ball on the undulating green, but what you might lose in your score, you will undoubtedly make up in the panoramic view of the course.

The clubhouse is atmospheric and wonderful, small rooms and lounges seeming to be set in a labyrinth that would perplex any Greek hero searching for the Minotaur. It is like

Golfers and caddies take on the rugged terrain at Porthcawl.

The eighteenth green and clubhouse at Porthcawl.

stepping back into the early twentieth century, and you can spend several happy hours either looking at the view or searching the honours boards for names you might recognise. No other clubhouse in Wales is nearer the sea than this quaint wooden building that was originally built for the Great Exhibition of 1851 – split into two, the other half went to Swansea Bay Golf Club where, as with Porthcawl, it is still in use. In the clubhouse, out on the course, history sits at your fingertips whenever you visit Royal Porthcawl.

## ABERDOVEY GOLF CLUB

Aberdovey Golf Club is one of the most scenic and enthralling courses in Wales. Founded in 1892, the course sits on the edge of the Dyfi Estuary in the southern part of Gwynedd and is a links course that is as picturesque as it is testing. It owes its origins to a group of local golf enthusiasts who, at the end of the Victorian era, decided to establish some holes on flat land outside town, then known as 'The Marsh'.

The young Bernard Darwin, perhaps the greatest of all British golf writers, spent much of his youth at Aberdovey and played the course many times. Indeed, he won the first tournament to take place at the course in April 1892, returning a gross score of 100. He wrote of Aberdovey that it was the links that 'my soul loves best of all the courses in the world.'

The course has been adapted and changed several times over the years, architects Braid and Colt both having had a hand in the eventual layout. You can feel their influence as you plot your way around this testing and demanding track.

A traditional links, the fairways at Aberdovey follow their narrow path out towards the sea and then back again. There is no such thing as an easy hole on this wonderful course, which has hosted many championships over the years.

The original clubhouse at Aberdovey.

A summer's day on the course at Aberdovey.

The clubhouse at Swansea Bay, modernised and updated.

## SWANSEA BAY GOLF CLUB

Having been founded in 1892, Swansea Bay Golf Club is the oldest club in the Swansea area. Just take one look at the magnificent clubhouse – the other half of the building being found at Royal Porthcawl – and you will automatically find yourself drawn back to the halcyon days of late-Victorian Britain when every club had caddies, travel to the courses was by horse-drawn brake, and the days of the feathery golf ball were only just past.

These days, modern transport systems have intruded somewhat and now the Swansea Bay golf course sits almost below the flyover on the M4 at Jersey Marine, four or five miles to the east of Swansea. The eighteen-hole layout is split in two by Fabian Way, the road leading from the motorway into Swansea.

The first half a dozen holes are flat, seeming to have a peaty base to them. Once across Fabian Way – you cross by a subway – the course follows the line of the estuary or river that runs up to Neath and the holes are pure links. Tight, narrow fairways are lined by bracken and gorse, most of them finishing with small greens that are difficult to hit and read. You cross back over the road to play the final few holes. This section of the course offers the only real climb, and there are more hedgerows and trees than on the links section.

As with all links courses, the wind and elements play a major factor at Swansea Bay. With just under half of the holes running along the side of the estuary, it does not have to blow very hard to make you realise that the course is exposed to whatever nature decides to throw its way.

## MONMOUTHSHIRE GOLF CLUB

Often wrongly referred to as Abergavenny Golf Club, the town nearest to the course, the Monmouthshire was founded in 1892. The first course was a nine-hole layout, and local legend declares that it came into existence following a bet – 'a golf course,' said someone, 'will never succeed in this area.' Thanks to a band of enthusiasts, including Lord Langattock

*Above:* The finishing line of the racecourse that once existed on Monmouthshire golf course.

*Left:* An aerial view of the course and clubhouse at Monmouthshire.

and Prime Minister Arthur Balfour, the course was laid out and a clubhouse created in a 500-year-old building that still functions as the clubhouse, even today.

The course has a stunning location, lying directly below the Blorenge Mountain and being overlooked by both Sugar Loaf and Skirrid Mountains. There can be very few prettier courses in Britain.

Monmouthshire is a parkland layout, the site once being a popular venue for horse racing. National Hunt Racing was held here for many years before the track was finally moved to Cheltenham in the 1870s. Interestingly, races continued to be held, even after the golf course was opened – there used to be a grandstand on the side of the river close to the present sixth tee, the finishing area for the races. Quite how golfers putting out on the green coped with the pounding of hooves and the roar of a frenzied crowd has not been recorded.

James Braid was brought in to design a full eighteen-hole course and this was opened in 1938. There has been considerable planting of trees over the years, something that has added to the quality and atmosphere of the course. There are six par threes at the Monmouthshire, all of them difficult, and one of them, the 230-yard sixteenth, has to be the club's signature hole. You drive off an elevated tee over the corner of a pond onto a green that is backed by tall, impressive trees. The course may not be long, but holes like this make it a fascinating test of golf.

## ASHBURNHAM GOLF CLUB

Founded in 1894, Ashburnham is the oldest golf club in Carmarthenshire. Situated at Burry Port to the west of Llanelli, this was originally a nine-hole layout being extended to eighteen in 1902, then further altered by J. H. Taylor and F. H. Hawtree in later years. The various designers each put something of their own style or stamp on the course and managed to succeed in creating a golfing work of art.

The course runs along the estuary, narrow fairways winding their way through sand dunes and dense scrub. When the wind howls in from Carmarthen Bay, this is possibly the

The golf course at Ashburnham.

Ashburnham clubhouse.

most rugged and exposed section of the Carmarthenshire coast, making Ashburnham one of the most demanding tests of golf you will ever find. Even the last hole, more parkland than links, required an accurate drive before turning sharply uphill towards the elevated green.

Ashburnham has staged many important tournaments, including the Home Internationals and Martini Championship. Sam Torrance won the 1976 Martini here, while Bernard Gallagher, former European Ryder Cup Captain, won his first professional event over the links in 1969. Harry Vardon claimed, 'Of all the courses in Wales, this is the one I like best.'

The clubhouse is an imposing building with views out over the course and nearby estuary. Take time to examine the dozens of honour boards around the various rooms and see if there are any names you can recognise. Ashburnham is a historic and famous golf course, one that no lover of the game should miss.

## NORTH WALES GOLF CLUB

The North Wales Golf Club was one of several courses founded in the late nineteenth century, partly to offer a service to holiday-makers in places like nearby Llandudno and Rhos-on-Sea. The course sits on the southern outskirts of Llandudno and offers spectacular views out towards Puffin Island and Anglesey.

The North Wales course lies next door to Maesdu Golf Club. However, whereas Maesdu has more of a parkland feel, North Wales is a typical links. The course is not long, being just over 6,000 yards, but you need to be accurate, as the fairways are narrow and the greens small. The rough is particularly punishing, being comprised mainly of heather and gorse, while deep bunkers defend several of the greens. When the wind blows, the best advice is to leave your driver in the bag – it is all too easy to see your shot suddenly picked up by the wind and swept away onto the next fairway or into the rough.

The rugged nature of the course at Llandudno can be seen on this early postcard view.

There are many fascinating holes here. The par five fifth, for example, is a dog-leg that takes you into the prevailing wind along a fairway that snakes like a roller-coaster. The beach is a real threat on several of the holes, particularly the par four eighth. This is a course that demands concentration.

## ROYAL ST DAVID'S, HARLECH

How many courses do you know of that are defended by the ruins of an imposing Norman castle? In Wales, there are several, but none is more spectacular than Royal St David's at Harlech. The castle stands up on the side of the hill and dominates the course as surely as the dunes and gorse. Its huge, imposing bulk is visible from all parts of the links.

Founded in 1894, the course lies on land that was once, back in the twelfth and thirteenth centuries, under water, being part of Cardigan Bay. In those days, the sea reached up and lapped at the walls of the castle. The sand and scrub left behind when the sea receded made a perfect setting for this glorious golf course. Prince Edward, later Edward VII, was patron to the club in its early days but the Royal Charter came several years later. In 1935, the Duke of Windsor, another Prince of Wales, became captain of the club, further extending the royal connections.

Not long by modern-day standards, Royal St David's has been called the toughest par 69 in the world. The fairways twist and turn through high sand dunes and typical links scrub grass. Play it on a calm day and the course is testing enough; play it on a wild and windswept afternoon, when the wind howls and the rain hammers down like metal rivets, it is virtually impossible. And yet, such is the quality of the place, you will undoubtedly love it, regardless of your score.

Only twice do successive holes take you in the same direction. There are only two par fives on the course whilst the par threes are some of the most difficult short holes you will

21

Harlech Castle dominates the course.

Unknown ladies playing Royal St David's, Harlech, in the 1920s.

Major Paul Norbury
driving from the first
tee at Harlech.

ever encounter. The eleventh is a real diamond, the green sitting in a nest of sand dunes, which really does mean that you hit the putting surface or die!

Although actually set on the edge of the course, the clubhouse environment is so all-embracing and the presence of the looming castle and rolling sand dunes so omnipresent, that you feel surrounded and encapsulated by a safety net – the atmosphere is like no other, anywhere in Wales.

The honours boards contain so many famous names, quite apart from the King, that you are inevitably caught up in the history of the place. How many can you spot – one clue: Sandy Lyle is there. If you intend to play golf in North Wales, do not ignore Royal St David's at Harlech.

## CARDIGAN GOLF CLUB

Cardigan Golf Club is situated on the west coast at Gwbert-on-Sea, high above Cardigan Bay, and is one of the great courses of Wales. Founded in 1895, the club was originally known as the Cardigan & Tivyside Golf Club but had difficulties in its early days and actually folded for a while. When the owners of the Cliff Hotel at Gwbert decided that they needed a course where visitors and locals could play, Cardigan Golf Club was re-established, being laid out by Mr Day, the club professional at Tenby, in 1902. A nine-hole course still exists at the hotel today.

In these early days, club members were transported to Gwbert in horse-drawn carriages, which were then stabled at the hotel while their games were played. The hotel offered clubhouse facilities at that time, but in November 1927, the club severed connections with the hotel and the links that had been built around it. Now known as Cardigan Golf Club a brand-new course was created just a few hundred yards up the road, on wonderfully springy and well-drained turf. In 1928, a small pavilion was built, and two years later, Leslie Mouland was appointed as Cardigan's first professional.

With the club increasing in popularity, the course was extended from nine to eighteen holes in the years after the Second World War. At 6,687 yards, at the time, this was considered a fairly long course, but the borrows on the greens and the twists and turns

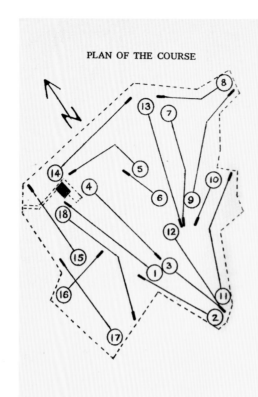

PLAN OF THE COURSE

# CARDIGAN GOLF CLUB

### GWBERT-ON-SEA

#### Cardigan 2035

##### LOCAL RULES

1. OUT OF BOUNDS. A ball is out of bounds when it is lying beyond the fences surrounding the course, in the surrounds of the Clubhouse, in the Car Park or on the Practice Putting Green.

2. The ruined cottage in the 11th fairway is an immovable obstruction. (Rule 31, 2 applies).

3. All young trees on the course are in ground under repair. Play prohibited. If a ball lies in an area of young trees it must be lifted and dropped within two club lengths of the nearest edge of the area of trees, not nearer the hole. No penalty.

4. A ball lying in a tractor mark may be treated as lying in ground under repair. (Rule 32 applies).

Temporary local rules will be shown on the Notice Board in the Clubhouse.

## MEN'S SCORE CARD

An early map and score card from Cardigan Golf Club.

The Cliff Hotel and its nine-hole golf course.

The sea is ever present at Cardigan Golf Club .

along bracken-bordered fairways have always meant that accuracy is more important than just standing up and trying to hit the ball as far as possible. The views off the top holes of the course are spectacular and will surely draw back any discerning golfer.

The club has continued to develop, hosting several championship and international events, and was winner of the inaugural Welsh Golf Club of the Year award.

## ST GILES GOLF CLUB, NEWTOWN

Although St Giles was originally founded in 1895, it only moved to its present location in 1908. The course now sits alongside the A483 on the outskirts of the mid-Wales town of Newtown and is bordered by the road to the south and by the River Severn to the north. This meandering stretch of water comes into play on three of the holes.

Harry Vardon, whilst working at nearby Llandrindod Wells, visited the course in 1911 and advised on some of the suggestions for development that were then being considered and talked about by members. As such, it can be properly called a 'Vardon-tweaked' course.

This is a nine-hole course, a parkland layout that uses the natural contours of the land, rising and falling towards the Severn. At just over 6,000 yards in length, it will provide a good test of golf for golfers of all ages and ability.

One of the interesting features of the course is the Gro Tump, an ancient motte-and-bailey castle dating from the early Norman incursions into the area in the twelfth century. Visitors will see this when they play the 'Pulpit', the par four third that is acknowledged as the hardest hole on the course. Cross a wooden bridge to an elevated tee and take a few minutes to view the old Norman Castle, one of the original fortifications put up after the Norman Conquest. Then forget history and get on with your game.

The fourth hole at St Giles, Newtown.

The motte of the old castle at St Giles.

## BORTH & YNYSLAS GOLF CLUB

Lying just ten miles to the north of Aberystwyth – and on the other side of the Dyfi Estuary from Aberdovey – Borth & Ynyslas, like Tenby and Pontnewydd, has claims to be the oldest club in Wales. Although Tenby has officially been granted that honour, members at Borth insist that they were in existence by 1885, some three or four years earlier.

The course sits on the margins of a fine, sandy beach amongst the Ynyslas dunes. It is one of the most enjoyable and picturesque courses in Wales, but when the wind blows in off the Irish Sea, this is a test of golf that will have players dredging for every ounce of skill they possess. One of the founder clubs of the Golf Union of Wales, this is a traditional links layout with many shared fairways. Harry Colt's 1940s redesign still survives, one of its main attractions being that it is on flat land and is, therefore, not physically demanding. This allows golfers of all ages and abilities to enjoy a spectacular location and golf of the highest quality.

The course has always been popular with locals and visitors alike. The coming of the Cambrian Railway in 1863 enabled the Aberystwyth area to enjoy fast links with the English Midlands, and as a result, Borth & Ynyslas developed and retained a high reputation as a centre for holiday golf. However, this is not just a holiday course, the Golf Union of Wales regularly choosing it as a venue for national and international tournaments.

When you consider the moguls, hillocks and sand traps that litter the fairways and guard the greens of Borth & Ynyslas – and then add in a howling wind that seems to blow both vertically and horizontally at the same time – this has to be one of the truly great links courses of Wales. Playing a round here is a rare experience, one not to be missed, whatever your handicap, whatever the state of your game.

The atmospheric links at Borth & Ynyslas.

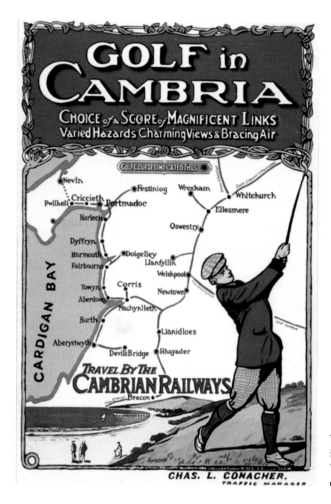

GOLF in CAMBRIA

CHOICE of a SCORE of MAGNIFICENT LINKS
Varied Hazards Charming Views & Bracing Air

GOLF COURSES INDICATED THUS ⦿

TRAVEL BY THE CAMBRIAN RAILWAYS

CHAS. L. CONACHER.
TRAFFIC MANAGER

The coming of the railway helped in the development of Borth & Ynyslas and several other courses on the West Wales coast.

## PENNARD GOLF CLUB

Founded in 1896, Pennard Golf Club lies just a dozen miles to the west of Swansea. It was constructed and laid out by James Braid and the course that you play today has changed very little from his original masterpiece of course design. It remains a relatively short layout, being just over 6,200 yards, but the rough, bracken, and roller-coaster-like fairways make this one of the most difficult golfing challenges in Wales.

Although designated a links, Pennard actually sits high up above the coast. And that means, in addition to all of the normal links-type hazards, there is invariably a strong breeze to contend with. Don't let that put you off the beauty of this course, which, at times, seems to contain no fairways and a distant flag or marker post is the only indication that safe haven awaits on the green ahead.

Many people have compared this links layout to that of the renowned Old Course at St Andrews. But Pennard is arguably more difficult than the original home of golf!

Be aware of the views available from the fairways of Pennard. Three Cliffs Bay, Oxwich Bay, and the ruins of Pennard Castle are just some of the spectacular visions awaiting you. And when you see the ponies roaming across the course – they have grazing rights here – think of them as part and parcel of the wonderful golfing experience.

The rugged links of Pennard.

The 1930s clubhouse at Pennard, destroyed by fire in the 1960s.

There are so many glorious holes at Pennard that it is difficult to pick out any one for particular mention. However, the short par threes are perhaps the pick of the bunch, as they will require accuracy, strength and more than a little imagination to play properly. Pennard has produced many great golfers over the years, none better than Vicki Thomas (even though she began her career at Bargoed). Vicki has represented Wales at every level and played in the Curtis Cup on many occasions.

If you had to choose just one links course in Wales, you could do a lot, lot worse than choose the wonderful Pennard Golf Club.

Rhos-on-Sea clubhouse.

An atmospheric view of the course at Rhos-on-Sea.

The golf links at Rhos-on-Sea.

## RHOS-ON-SEA GOLF CLUB

Rhos-on-Sea Golf Club, founded in 1899, was one of many clubs to benefit from the coming of the railways. It was originally created to offer quality golf to the Victorian ladies and gentlemen who came sweeping into the area from the industrial belt of the Midlands.

The course lies on The Promenade in Rhos-on-Sea, just two miles to the west of Colwyn Bay. It is situated within walking distance of the town centre and the hotels and boarding houses where these summer visitors would stay. In the years after the turn of the nineteenth century, the course quickly established itself as something of a 'Mecca' for holiday golfers, something that has never changed, although the place has always remained popular with the locals as well.

Rhos-on-Sea Golf Club was and still is a parkland course, despite lying close to the sea and offering golfers more than a little 'whiff of ozone'. It is relatively flat with only a few small climbs, therefore being ideal for players of all abilities. At 5,612 yards in length, this is not a long course, but its par of 68 (SS 68) will ensure that players will be tested and, to employ the old golfing cliché, use 'every club in their bag'. The greens are flat and true but will repay accurate observation and a firm putting stroke.

As you would expect from a course lying close to the sea, there are some fabulous views along the coast towards the Little and the Great Orme. In the other direction, you can pick out the towns of Prestatyn and Rhyl.

## MORLAIS CASTLE GOLF CLUB

Morlais Castle Golf Club owes its origin to the time when six friends, who used to take a regular Sunday walk across the Bryniau above Merthyr Tydfil, became infected by the 'golf

The sweeping contours of Morlais Castle golf course.

One of the greens at Morlais Castle.

Women at Morlais Castle Golf Club, *c.* 1900.

bug'. They decided to buy some clubs and balls, sank some jam jars as holes at various places along their walk and proceeded to enjoy their games. It was 1900 and in this manner the game of golf came to Morlais Castle.

When other friends and local people also became interested in these 'jam jar walks', a meeting was called, a committee voted in, and the club came into being. Originally a nine-hole course, Scotsman David Tate was taken on as club professional in 1903. He helped design and improve the nine holes. The Dowlais Iron Company donated a wooden building, and this functioned as a clubhouse for many years, being extended many times.

In 1989, an additional nine holes was built, and five years later, a brand-new clubhouse was added. Due to the developments in equipment design, by the final years of the twentieth century, it was clear that further extensions were needed for the course. It is now a testing and demanding eighteen-hole moorland track that is also scenically attractive, and when the wind blows, one that will make you concentrate hard throughout your round.

There are not many courses in Wales that exist in the shadow of old Norman castles. Royal St David's is one, Morlais Castle is another. Built by Gilbert de Clare in the thirteenth century, the ruins of the old fortification lie alongside the third fairway and help make this a very narrow driving hole. Atmosphere and a serious test of golf – what more could any golfer want?

# THE NEW CENTURY
# 1901 TO 1910

The year 1901 marked not just the beginning of a new century but, perhaps more significantly, the end of one era and the start of a new one. Early in the year, Queen Victoria died and was succeeded by her son, Edward VII. Victoria had reigned for so long that many people had never known a different monarch and her name and all she stood for have since become synonymous with the second half of the nineteenth century.

But now, at the beginning of the new century, the Queen had suddenly gone, and to many, it seemed as if a whole new world was opening up – a new king, a new century, a new outlook on life. As if to mark the moment, in 1903, King Edward's son, now the new Prince of Wales, agreed to become patron of the Welsh Golfing Union, a great boost to the standing of the sport in the Principality.

With victory in the Boer War, the British Empire, despite the knocks it had taken in the early years of the conflict, had regained its position as the most important military and economic force in the world. And back home, more and more people were beginning to enjoy the benefits of that empire.

In Wales, there was a huge surge in golf club membership – and in the creation of new golf clubs. The working classes were still, by and large, excluded from the game – apart from being employed as caddies or, if they were lucky, having an Artisans Section, as they did at Southerndown – but for those who had money, it was time to bask in the easy splendour of Edwardian Britain. For most people in the middle and upper classes, it really did seem as if the good times would never end.

Yet, even as early as 1901, storm clouds were gathering, and if people had only known it, this last burst of Edwardian sunlight would soon be ended by the guns of 1914.

## RADYR GOLF CLUB

Radyr Golf Club, founded in 1902, sits in the village of Radyr, just five miles north of Cardiff. It is the oldest of all the Cardiff golf clubs, coming into existence when the Lisvane Golf Club (soon to become Llanishen) folded and a group of members decided to create a new club. Suitable land was found at Radyr and the long history of the club began.

The original wooden clubhouse was destroyed by fire in 1913. It was replaced by the existing building, which was designed in two sections so that, if the club was ever dissolved, it could be sold as a pair of semi-detached houses. Such a move, cautious and pragmatic at the same time, undoubtedly reflected the make-up of members in these early days.

Radyr is a parkland course, albeit one with a few steep climbs and drops. The finishing hole is a classic example of this, a straight drive being needed to take you to the top of the hill before dropping sharply down to a sunken green close to the front of the clubhouse. The course winds its way across and around hillsides, through banks of tall, mature trees. Ditches, hedges and the occasional stretch of water provide other hazards that golfers might find it better to avoid.

The course was designed by Harry Colt, one of only three full Colt courses to be found in Wales. If the quality of the course isn't enough to keep you enthralled – and, frankly, we

*Right:* Golf in the new century.

*Below:* Wild and rugged, golf in the early twentieth century was still a sport for the upper classes.

doubt that – there are some fabulous views of Cardiff and the Severn Estuary beyond. This is a great place to play golf.

## BRECON GOLF CLUB

Brecon Golf Club can be found on the outskirts of the town of Brecon and came into existence in 1902. Designed by James Braid, it is one of the finest nine-hole courses in the country. Apart from the first, a steep uphill par three, the course is set on flat land that provides easy walking, offering glorious views of the flanking Brecon Beacons.

The golf clubhouse at Radyr, later destroyed by fire.

The golf links at Radyr.

The club has recently changed some of its layout, bringing the second green back some yards, for example. This has made the hole somewhat safer, but it has in no way damaged the quality of the golf on offer. And the view from so many of the fairways remains dramatic and enthralling.

Most of the fairways are bordered by tall trees and mature hedges – difficult enough in the winter but doubly hard when trees and hedges are in full bloom. The River Usk flows along the northern flank of the course and provides a wonderful backdrop to the sixth hole when you feel as if you are hitting into the middle of the fiver.

The course at Brecon, viewed from over the River Usk.

Brecon is a long-established course with an honourable tradition, being only the tenth club to join the Welsh Golf Union. This parkland layout has good drainage and is playable throughout the year.

## ST DAVID'S CITY GOLF CLUB, PEMBROKESHIRE

St David's City Golf Club in Pembrokeshire lies just a few minutes away from Britain's smallest city. It occupies a spectacular position overlooking Whitesand Bay, Ramsey Sound, and the deadly 'Bitches Rocks', where, in 1910, the local lifeboat was wrecked. There can be relatively few golf courses that occupy a more scenic setting than St David's, a true Welsh gem if ever there was one.

The club was founded in 1903, although there had been proposals to create a golf course in the area several years before when it was planned to run a new rail link to St David's. In the event, the railway ventured no further than Letterston, but the club duly came into existence shortly after the turn of the century. The course was purported to be laid out by Dr Williams and Colonel Bleddyn Rees, and by 1905, a green fee of one shilling a day was being levied.

During the Second World War, the course was closed, topsoil and sand being taken away for use in the armament depot at Trecwn. When the club reformed after the war, the whole area was a mass of weeds, brambles and rocks. Nevertheless, members rallied around, and it was not long before the course was in play again.

St David's City Golf Club has to be one of the most atmospheric of all Welsh courses. It might only be nine holes, but they are nine of the most beautiful holes you will ever encounter. On a summer morning, with the wind fresh off the sea, the view from these fairways alone is worth the price of a green fee, never mind the golf.

*Left:* The fifth tee at St David's in Pembrokeshire; Dr Williams driving.

*Below:* Beautiful views of the Pembrokeshire coastline are found on almost every hole of the St David's course.

## NEWPORT GOLF CLUB, GWENT

Lying three miles to the north-west of Newport in the village of Rogerstone, Newport Golf Club came into existence in 1903, when a club was founded at Lady Hill to the east of the town. When, in 1912, a better site became available in the Rogerstone area, a small group of members left Lady Hill with a view to creating their own course and Newport Golf Club was born.

Long known as one of the best inland courses in the country, Newport has hosted many important tournaments. These include the Women's Home Internationals, the Welsh Professional Championships, and the Great Oak Amateur Championship. This is a fine parkland course measuring nearly 6,500 yards. There are no real climbs on the course, although the fairways are undulating and are flanked by thick woodlands. The eleventh is one of Newport's classic holes, where the ball has to be driven through a narrow avenue of trees that run for the full length of the hole. Be straight or perish!

One of the sweeping fairways at Newport Golf Club.

*Above left:* Pat Roberts, many times ladies' champion at Newport Golf Club.

*Above right:* Paul Mayo, British Amateur Champion and Walker Cup player.

Golfers on the old course at Tredegar Park.

The club has produced many fine players over the years, none more so than the current club professional, Paul Mayo. As an amateur, he won the British Youth's Championship, the Amateur Championship, and was the leading amateur in the 1987 Open. He played in the Walker Cup before becoming a successful European Tour player for several years. Welsh woman international Pat Roberts won the Ladies' Club Championship here so many times that it is almost impossible to count.

Newport is a great golf course, one that any visitor should include on their itinerary.

## TREDEGAR PARK GOLF CLUB

The history of Tredegar Park Golf Club is one of triumph over adversity, as the club has been forced to change its location on a number of occasions. Originally founded as Lady Hill Golf Club in 1903, golf was played until 1922, when the land was required for development. As a result, the Lady Hill Golf Club split apart, some members going on to join Newport Golf Club, others choosing to stay with the rump of the old club and form Tredegar Park.

Viscount Tredegar, first president of the club, donated part of his Deer Park, close to Tredegar House in Newport, and the course was laid out. The springy nature of the turf was ideal for golf, and by 1935, Tredegar Park boasted some of the most attractive holes in South Wales. Three of these were on hilly ground, the other fifteen on land that meandered through tall trees, often following a fast-flowing river.

When the M4 motorway was built in the 1960s, the club lost its 'elevated' holes. However, the course was adjusted and play continued, the final two holes – stunning and delightful par threes – providing a wonderful finishing stretch.

The club was forced to move again in 1999 to its present site at Parc-y-Brain Road in Rogerstone when the land at Tredegar Park was required for supposed redevelopment – something that has not yet happened. The current course is long and demanding with sweeping holes that wander across the hills to the north of the M4 motorway.

A panoramic view of Langland Bay golf course.

The tricky sixteenth at Langland Bay.

## LANGLAND BAY GOLF CLUB

Langland Bay is something of a hybrid, part parkland, part seaside links, situated to the west of Swansea on the edge of the Gower Peninsula. Founded in 1904, the course offers magnificent views of Gower and of the Bristol Channel.

Being, in the main, set high up on the hills above the Channel, wind is always going to be an issue on this course, particularly on holes like the par four sixth, which is renowned as one of the toughest holes on the Gower Coast. None of the other holes are particularly easy either, and some, like the eighth, where you drive off what seems to be the side of a cliff, are nothing short of magnificent.

The par three sixteenth is called 'Death or Glory'. There is no fairway and the hole is bordered on the right by the Bristol Channel, on the left by a steep hundred-foot bank. You really do need to hit the green or simply pull another ball from your bag.

Langland Bay golf course features plenty of rough, and many sand traps. The greens are not large, and accuracy is a crucial factor in any game here. It is all too easy to lose concentration in the face of some of the best views on the Welsh coast. Sometimes it is easier to keep your head down and forget the sights – but then again, that spoils your enjoyment of one of the best courses in the country.

## CRICCIETH GOLF CLUB

Say Criccieth to most people, and they will respond 'Lloyd George'. The Welsh wizard and British Prime Minister during the First World War may well have come from the area, but Criccieth also boasts one of the most interesting and most under-rated golf courses in the Principality.

The clubhouse at Criccieth Golf Club.

*Golf Pavilion and 18th Hole, Criccieth*

The eighteenth hole at Criccieth – note the square green.

Founded in 1905, Criccieth Golf Club lies about a mile inland from the town of Criccieth and offers stunning views along the Llyn Peninsula, down towards Criccieth Castle and out over the sea. The peaks of the Snowdon Mountain range loom like fists of steel in the background, louring darkly on gloomy days, sparkling like early-morning raindrops in the springtime. As club members will tell you, it is all too easy to concentrate on the views to the detriment of your game.

This is a unique eleven-hole golf course, mountain top in style and with several quirky but testing holes. The last two, in particular, are worthy of note. For the penultimate hole, the green lies 70 feet above you – hit this one in two and you will really be playing well. In contrast, the final hole is a par three where the green lies 100 feet below the tee, a spectacular way to finish your round.

Criccieth boasts the unusual distinction of having three British Prime Ministers once play a round of golf together on its fairways. The men in question were David Lloyd George (who regularly played here), Winston Churchill, and Andrew Bonar Law. Hallowed footsteps indeed! Criccieth offers a totally different experience from the nearby links courses like Royal St David's and Pwllheli.

## SOUTHERNDOWN GOLF CLUB

Southerndown has been described as 'a unique course, near to the sea, with entrancing views'. Situated on the cliffs above Ogmore in South Glamorgan and founded in 1905, this course really is a links in the sky. Willie Fernie designed the original course, while Harry Vardon and James Braid both worked on amendments, before Willie Park, Harry Colt and Donald Steel all had their say in the eventual layout that we see today.

*Above:* A classic view of the gorse-covered slopes at Southerndown Golf Club.

*Left:* Playing out of the gorse at Southerndown is always a hazard.

Gorse-lined fairways, deep valleys, blind drives, and a wind that whistles in off the sea – these invariably combine to make a round at Southerndown one of the most satisfying and interesting rounds of golf you will ever play. Only rarely is there a level lie on these fairways, and part of the joy – masochistic as it might be – is to watch your ball bounce unexpectedly off a mound or hillock and end up further off line than you would ever have dreamt possible.

Trying to play to the green with gorse bushes pricking at your trouser legs is all part of Southerndown's charm. So, too, are the resident sheep, which have grazing rights on the

Southerndown, thronged with spectators, during the 1968 Martini Championship.

course. They will tell you, in the clubhouse, the story of one member who topped his ball into the rear end of one of these sheep – which then took off and deposited the said ball on the green, nicely close to the hole!

Home to the Duncan dynasty, one of the most influential families in Welsh golf, Southerndown has held many great championships. These include the Piccadilly Masters, the Martini International, and the Duncan Putter, which takes place every Easter. The course also featured in the *Shell's Wonderful World of Golf* television programme in the 1950s. Bernard Darwin, arguably the greatest golf writer of all time, called Southerndown his favourite course in the whole of Britain. You cannot get a better recommendation than that.

## PRESTATYN GOLF CLUB

Prestatyn Golf Club in Denbighshire is the most northerly golf course in mainland Wales (not counting Anglesey) and is a links layout that runs along the foreshore of Barkby Beach. Fred Collins of Llandudno designed the original nine holes in 1905, but the course was soon extended, and a full eighteen holes was ready for play by 1906.

The history of the club has been rather chequered. In 1921, the original nine holes were taken for development, a new nine being constructed the following year. In 1921, Stradbrook House was converted into a clubhouse and was used until 1945 as both the clubhouse and as a hotel where visitors to the area, golfers and non-golfers alike, could stay for a few days' break. Following the death of Lord Aberconway, the course and hotel had to be sold to pay death duties, and in 1960, the club was given notice to quit. However, compulsory purchase by Prestatyn Council saved the club, and in 1972, a new clubhouse was built.

One feature of this course is the Prestatyn Gutter, a canal that crosses the links and has been the *bête noire* of many golfers. There are no easy holes on this course, many of the fairways being lined by huge sand hills and tufts of sea grass. When the wind comes in off the Irish Sea, this can be one of the hardest courses in Wales, with greens that are true but tricky to read. And the clubhouse is a wonderful sanctuary once your round is over.

Prestatyn course, clubhouse, and beach.

## LLANDRINDOD WELLS GOLF CLUB

When Harry Vardon arrived to plan and map out a golf course on the hills above Llandrindod Wells in 1905, the Edwardian Spa town was in the heyday of its popularity. Vardon simply made the steep climb up the hill and found himself confronted by a plateau of moor and heathland one thousand feet above sea level. There was not really an awful lot for Vardon to do. Almost immediately, he knew this was perfect golfing country.

The course meanders across the top of a plateau. Only two holes can be described as hilly, the first being a real lung-buster. But once you are up at the top of the climb, the views are spectacular and the gorse-covered fairways are a delight to behold. In the springtime, several of the holes are lined by wonderfully evocative swathes of bluebells.

There are many marvellous holes here, but the 297-yard eighteenth has to be one of the best. It's short for a par four but much of the carry is across deep rough, a valley and a ravine. Of course, you can hit the green in one – you can also top it down into the depths and from there, really, there is no way out.

One interesting fact about Llandrindod Wells – there are no bunkers on the course. The sand would simply blow away in the wind. However, there are plenty of other hazards, ranging from trees and valleys to gorse and thick rough. The club was, for many years, home to the Welsh Boys' Championships, and interestingly, its opening was marked by a match between members of the great Triumvirate – Vardon, Braid, and J. H. Taylor.

## CAERPHILLY GOLF CLUB

There are a variety of ways to arrive at a golf club – by bus, by foot, by car. But by an aeroplane? Well, the pilot was not actually going to Caerphilly for a game of golf, he was just landing his First World War aircraft on the first fairway after getting into some difficulties in the skies above Caerphilly.

The remote nature of Llandrindod Wells Golf Club can be glimpsed in this early postcard view.

The clubhouse at Llandrindod Wells.

One of the greens at Caerphilly, cut square and bordered by wire to keep out livestock.

Caerphilly Golf Club was founded in 1905, the moving spirit being Charles Stuart Goodfellow. He had been down to Minehead on holiday in 1902 when he came across people playing golf on the sands and decided he would like to take up the game himself. A nine-hole course was duly laid out on the farmlands of Pencapel on Caerphilly Mountain, and this early layout remained in play until extension of the course began in 1963. Further extensions, with several new holes, took place in the early 2000s and the course now comprises a full eighteen holes.

It would be wrong to say the Caerphilly is an easy walk, because there are several fierce climbs, notably on the early holes. But once you reach the top of the course, you will find some of the most spectacular views imaginable – towards the Brecon Beacons in the north and, in particular, down towards the town's famous Norman Castle, the largest in Wales and certainly one of the most spectacular sets of ruins you are ever likely to find.

It is worth braving the hills for the views and the quality of the course. Thick rough and mountain grass mean that accuracy is crucial – at least until you reach the lower portions of the course. Caerphilly will repay any discerning golfer.

## HOLYWELL GOLF CLUB

Holywell Golf Club was founded in 1906. Although sitting nearly a thousand feet above sea level, like Southerndown, the course has been described as 'a links in the air'. The natural contours on the course certainly demand links-style play with a chip and a run often being preferable to a high lobbed shot.

Holywell began its life as a nine-hole course before being extended to a full eighteen in 1926. Just over ten years later, however, the club lost nine of its hole during the Second World War 'Dig for Victory' campaign. Members continued to play the nine holes until May 1991 when the club finally managed to acquire a further nine holes to bring it back to a full layout.

The eighth green at Hoylwell.

An early view of Holywell golf course.

As with many Welsh golf clubs, for several years, no play was allowed at Holywell on Sundays. Even when this regulation was relaxed, two or three of the holes that ran close to the local church were ruled out of play on the Sabbath during service times.

There are many great holes at Holywell, the fifteenth probably being the club's signature hole. It is a daunting and intimidating par three that takes you over the remains of an old quarry onto a green that slopes from back to front. The final hole is another classic, your drive taking you down a narrow fairway with out-of-bounds on the right and thick heather on the left.

## WREXHAM GOLF CLUB

Many courses have changed location over the years, but Wrexham Golf Club has had no fewer than six different homes. The club owes its origins to the closure of Gresford Golf Club in 1906 when the land on which the course was situated was taken to sink Gresford Colliery. Several members then created Gwersyllt Park Golf Club, which in due course made the move to the present location at Borras. James Braid designed the new course, which ran as an eighteen-hole layout from 1923.

Driving off at Wrexham.

A 1960s view of Wrexham's clubhouse.

During the Second World War, in 1940, the club was ordered to block its fairways with machinery and other obstacles in order to prevent enemy aircraft landing, something that undoubtedly made play difficult! More serious, however, was the eventual loss of half of the land in order to build a fighter base to protect the Merseyside area. After that, play was restricted to just nine holes, and this continued to be the case until 1950, when fourteen holes became available, building or rebuilding to a full eighteen in due course.

One incident of note during the wartime years was the crash of a Halifax Bomber on the incline between the first and second fairways. No casualties were involved. Part of the present second fairway is now built on the runway of the old aerodrome and this can still be picked out in dry summer weather.

Wrexham is a parkland course where tall trees blend easily into the landscape, but all of which play an important part in how the golfer approaches each hole. A base of sand and gravel makes this a well-drained course so that it is playable all year round. The fairways are undulating with one or two steep climbs to test you physically, and several of the holes have out-of-bounds that require careful management if you are not to find yourself in serious trouble.

The course has hosted many important championship events but is not unduly long. This can be deceptive as there are enough problems here to catch out any unwary golfer. Wrexham Golf Club is easily reached, lying just two miles to the east of the town on the A534 to Nantwich.

Discussing their round, members and Mr Marjoram, the club pro, at West Mon Golf Club in 1911.

## WEST MONMOUTHSHIRE GOLF CLUB

Located just outside Nantyglo, West Monmouthshire Golf Club sits in the heart of 'Alexander Cordell' country. Just a few miles down the valley, you will find the location for his famous book *Rape of the Fair Country,* and the remains of the iron and coal industries are ever present.

The course was founded in 1906 on a layout designed by Ben Sayers and constructed by a group of local schoolteachers and doctors. It was extended to a full eighteen holes in 1909, being described as a heathland course. Gorse, scrub grass and water are just some of the challenges that await you on this course, which you feel looks exactly like it would have done a hundred years ago.

Yet it is the elements that offer the biggest challenge here. A round of golf could see you battling with wind, rain and hail before the sun suddenly and miraculously emerges. West Mon, as it is universally known, boasts the highest tee in Britain. This is the fourteenth tee, standing at 1,518 feet above sea level – it is well worth pausing at this spot to take in the views of the surrounding valleys and hills.

West Mon provides a very different challenge from many of the manicured parkland courses in the south. Play this one well and you can be very pleased with yourself indeed. Craig Evans, one of the best amateur Welsh internationals of the last twenty years, still plays out of West Mon, relishing the challenge of these rugged and demanding fairways.

## NEFYN & DISTRICT GOLF CLUB

There is no other way to describe it – Nefyn & District Golf Club is, quite simply, the most dramatic and spectacular links location in Wales. This particularly applies to the holes out on the peninsula where the fairways are narrow and it seems that there is nothing to stop

The course at
Morfa Nefyn.

The clubhouse
at Morfa Nefyn,
in use for the
General Meeting
of the North Wales
Advertising Board,
September 1923.

your ball plummeting into the water below. This section of the course has to be the most photographed piece of golfing topography in Wales. Unfortunately, the peninsula holes are only rarely in play, which is something of a shame as to stride along these cliff-top fairways is an experience not to be missed.

Nefyn & District Golf Club was founded on the headland at Porthdinllaen in Gwynedd in the spring and early summer of 1907. James Braid was the architect, and he designed a magnificent course with no fewer then ten of the holes running alongside the sea. In the early days, members consisted of a cross section of locals, holiday visitors, and people temporarily employed in the area.

Several new holes were designed and inaugurated in 1993, as an addendum to the spectacular fairways along the adjacent peninsula. Even this adjustment does not detract from the overall experience of playing at Nefyn & District. And who knows, when you visit, the peninsula holes just might be in play. Even if they are not, you should take time to walk up there and enjoy the views across the sea to Anglesey and, down below, pick out Porthdinllaen, a village that lies on the sea's edge and has been preserved by the National Trust.

The golf course and bay at Abersoch.

GOLF COURSE AND SANDS, BENARE HEAD, ABERSOCH          W 6757

Players on the links at Abersoch.

GOLF LINKS, ABERSOCH.

## ABERSOCH GOLF CLUB

Abersoch Golf Club lies half a mile to the south of the town of Abersoch on the Llyn Peninsula and offers a combination of links and parkland golf. It was founded in 1907 and was one of several North Wales courses to benefit from the advent of the tourist trade. Originally a nine-hole course, designed by Harry Vardon, Abersoch has been extended and now offers golfers a full eighteen holes.

Sandy soil, a unique microclimate and fast draining sand dunes give Abersoch a robust constitution. Nobody can remember the last time the course was fully closed because of the weather. And yet it is an attractive and compelling course that offers a wide range of challenge.

Here the golfer will find all types of hazard, ranging from sand dunes and gorse bushes to tall trees and ditches that snake across part of the course. At just under 6,000 yards, Abersoch is not long and offers easy walking. Yet underestimate this course at your peril. It will repay cautious play and accuracy with iron clubs. Abersoch remains an essential part of any golfing experience on the Llyn Peninsula.

MOEL FAMMAU FROM GOLF COURSE, PANT-Y-MWYN. W.5267.

The rolling fairways of Mold golf course.

## MOLD GOLF CLUB

Mold Golf Club was first established on Hafod Moor outside the town in 1905, but some four years later, the club was transferred, first to Padeswood and then, in 1928, to Pantymwyn. Most people regard the year 1909 as the moment in time that the course and club were truly established. As such, it remains one of the oldest courses in Flintshire.

In the early days, a second-hand cricket pavilion acted as a clubhouse, and by some miracle, this wooden structure survived the various moves, remaining in use until the late 1960s. Disaster hit the club in the 1950s and 1970s when the second green collapsed and, during a gale, the clubhouse roof was blown off. Mold Golf Club survived these setbacks, being extended to a full eighteen holes in 1978.

The course is not long, being just over 5,500 yards in length, but with plenty of rough and mature trees bordering the fairways, it offers a definite challenge to golfers of all abilities.

## CAERNARFON GOLF CLUB

Caernarfon is very much a royal town, being the scene of the Investiture of the Prince of Wales in 1969. So it is fitting that the town boasts one of the oldest and best courses in North Wales. The original course at Dinas Dinlle was opened in 1906, about three and a half miles from the town, but in less than a year, the club had closed, as its location was virtually inaccessible.

There was no golf at Caernarfon for over two years, until a meeting was held in September 1909 to discuss the possibility of founding a new club. Tourists were increasingly coming to the town and, it was felt, a new golf club would be beneficial to both visitors and locals. Before long, sixty acres of land bordering the Menai Straits was leased and a new nine-hole course laid out. The first competitions were held over Easter weekend in 1910, and a year later, two famous politicians, David Lloyd George and Winston Churchill, played on the course whilst in Caernarfon to make arrangements for the 1911 Investiture of the Prince of Wales.

Well defined and well maintained, this aerial view of Caernarfon golf course also shows the town and castle in the background.

The old clubhouse and one of the original members of Caernarfon Golf Club.

The original clubhouse was destroyed by fire in December 1911 and a new one built at a cost of £400. During the First World War, the fairways were turned back to agriculture and the club was dissolved. The original course at Dinas Dinlle had been reopened in 1913, and this appears to have been played during the war years. In 1919, new land was obtained close to the Aber Bridge. The club was re-founded, and for a while, the small tower that overlooked it became a temporary clubhouse. In due course, a new clubhouse was built and more land obtained in order to extend the course to a full eighteen holes. The new layout was ready by the spring of 1981.

Today, Caernarfon Golf Club is a thriving and popular venue for golf in north-west Wales, more than capable of holding its own against courses like Nefyn and Llandudno.

## PENMAENMAWR GOLF CLUB

Situated just a short drive from Conwy, off the A55 Express Way, Penmaenmawr Golf Club lies in a valley below Moel Llys. In fact, the course can boast three separate mountains as a backdrop, while, in front, the golfer gazes out towards Anglesey on one side and the Great Orme on the other.

There are several slopes on this mountain-style course, but the views more than make up for any energy expended. It has fine, springy turf, which invariably beautifully sets up the ball for your second shot. The rough is not overly thick, but there are plenty of hazards. Notable amongst these are the dry-stone walls that bisect the fairways, particularly on the second, seventh, and sixteenth holes. There is no par five on the course, but the sweeping contours of the ground will provide plenty of other challenges.

Several of the greens here are elevated and therefore require accurate approach shots. The greens themselves demand careful reading if you are going to hit anywhere close to your handicap. Penmaenmawr offers spectacular views and golf that will challenge you, whatever your age, whatever your ability.

Surrounded by hills, Penmaenmawr golf course.

## DOLGELLAU GOLF CLUB

For those in the know, Dolgellau Golf Club is renowned as one of perhaps half a dozen 'hidden gems' of Welsh golf. It is a nine-hole course located just outside the town of Dolgellau in Gwynedd and lies on what used to be the hunting grounds of Llewellyn, the last true and native-born Prince of Wales.

Mature oak and holly trees add to the character of this undulating parkland layout, making it one of the most attractive inland courses in the country. The course was founded in 1910 and celebrates its centenary in 2010, the year that the Ryder Cup comes to Wales.

Although only nine holes, there are different tee positions if you wish to play a second nine. Accuracy and control are far more important than length, but the course will reward the brave approach onto small and deceptive greens.

Dolgellau Golf Club is overlooked by the looming bulk of Cader Idris. It makes an impressive backdrop. The top six holes provide spectacular views out over the Mawddach Estuary and beyond towards the Irish Sea. Pay a visit to this one and you will surely understand the epithet 'hidden gem'.

## ABERGELE GOLF CLUB

Set in the magnificent grounds of Gwrych Castle, a nineteenth-century folly or mock castle built by the Countess of Dundonald, Abergele Golf Club was founded in 1910. The original course was laid out on land owned by the Dundonald estate, but in 1942, with Britain engaged in fighting for its life against Nazi Germany, approximately twenty acres were ploughed up as part of the 'Dig for Victory' campaign.

In 1968, the club moved to its present location, ninety acres of parkland being purchased from the estate by the members. The new course was designed by Hawtree & Sons, the renowned golf architects and course designers – and what a job they made of it. The new course at Abergele lies close to the sea and offers what many have described as 'heart-stopping' views of the coastal plain and of the rolling Welsh hills.

The course itself meanders its way through groves of tall trees, and the fairways, although flat, are bordered by considerable amounts of rough. Bushes and trees might well add to the beauty of this parkland course, but they are also a real hazard to play around when they are in full bloom.

The course measures just over 6,500 yards and with an SS of 71 provides a challenge that will make all golfers think about their shots. Always well maintained and manicured, this is one of the most interesting courses in Denbighshire and is well worth playing if you should ever find yourself on this stretch of the North Wales coast.

## BARGOED GOLF CLUB

Bargoed Golf Club was founded in 1910, an eighteen-hole mountain-parkland course that is located in the town of Bargoed, twenty miles north of Cardiff. Originally, the club was known as the East Glamorgan Golf Club and only changed its name at the end of the 1920s. The course is not unduly hilly, although there are some short, stiff pulls that will leave you quite breathless if you are not too careful.

Bargoed is a relatively short course, measuring just over 6,000 yards, but every hole requires accuracy and, occasionally, length off the tee if you are going to hit the green in regulation. There is a crossover on two occasions and you need to take care, but this only adds to the quirkiness of the course. The first hole is an interesting par four where the green

The beautiful nine-hole course at Dolgellau.

The ninth green at Dolgellau.

Overlooked by the castle, Abergele golf course waits for visitors.

Spectacular views towards the Brecon Beacons from Bargoed golf course.

Two of Bargoed's finest, Denise Richards (left) and Vicki Thomas (right) along with author Trudy Carradice during the Senior Ladies' Home Internationals, 2007.

is bounded by a stone wall – take an iron in order to get a look at the green with your second shot; you take on the green with your drive at your own peril.

The panoramic views from the course are spectacular, particularly when you gaze up the Deri Valley towards the Brecon Beacons. On a crisp winter morning or an early spring day, there can be no finer place to stand and contemplate life. The course itself has a number of tall trees that border the fairways, the last three holes in particular being lined by foliage that inevitably seems destined to catch your ball.

Bargoed has produced many fine players over the years, none better than the Rawlings sisters, Kerri, Mandy and Vicki. All of them played for Wales at various levels, and Vicki, now Thomas after her marriage, represented Britain in the Curtis Cup on three occasions. Other internationals include Denise Richards (now the club secretary), Lucy Gould, and David Price.

# TO THE FIRST WORLD WAR AND BEYOND: 1911 TO 1919

The second decade of the twentieth century was a difficult period for Welsh golf clubs, due mainly to the outbreak of the Great War in 1914. This conflict devastated Europe and caused 10 million deaths between 1914 and 1918. Even after the Treaty of Versailles ended the war and returned the world to peace, people had little inclination to start spending money on the creation of new golf clubs. They had survived the war, now it was time to survive its after-effects. It was hardly a time for frivolous pastimes like playing golf.

The previous decade had seen an incredible boom in the number of golf clubs founded in Wales, but almost on cue, as soon as 1910 closed, things began to change.

Several courses had already been planned and designed. For these, there was no option but to continue with the development. However, new ideas, new courses? That was different, and even in 1911, the war clouds were already beginning to gather as people's eyes were starting to turn towards the threat provided by the Kaiser and his military regime.

Several clubs were brought into existence between 1911 and 1914, but only two, Whitchurch in Cardiff and Llandudno (Maesdu), during the war years. This paucity seems to sum up the decade.

## ABERYSTWYTH GOLF CLUB

Harry Vardon designed Aberystwyth Golf Club just before the First World War in 1911 when the town was enjoying something of a tourist boom. The course sits high on a hill at the northern end of the town, above the university and adjacent to the famous Cliff Railway.

The last three holes are situated above and behind the atmospheric clubhouse, the views off the seventeenth offering a wonderful perspective of Aberystwyth town and promenade below you. There are glorious views off every single hole but don't let that put you off your game. The course may be superbly maintained, but this is deceptive, as you would expect with any Vardon-designed course, and it will catch out anybody who is not concentrating.

The course is not unduly long but most of the par fours play like par fives – this particularly applies to the first couple of holes, which take you steadily up hill. The course is described as meadowland/parkland, but when the wind blows in off the Irish Sea, you could be forgiven for thinking that you were playing on a links. Water, ditches, bunkers, and trees provide plenty of traps to catch the unwary golfer.

There is not a bad hole on the course, each one offering a different type of challenge. But, strangely enough, the gem of Aberystwyth probably lies in its clubhouse. It looks as if it had been dragged out of the late 1800s and is surely one of the most attractive clubhouse buildings anywhere in Wales.

## HOLYHEAD GOLF CLUB

Situated at the northern end of Holy Island and connected to the main part of Anglesey by a causeway, Holyhead Golf Club was founded in 1912. Designed by James Braid, this layout is a

*Left:* Elegance and exercise on the golf course.

*Below:* By 1911, golf was becoming increasingly popular.

5462. MAES-DU GOLF LINKS. LLANDUDNO. — JUDGES' LTD.

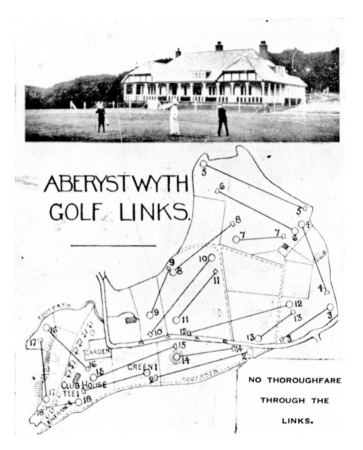

ABERYSTWYTH
GOLF LINKS.

NO THOROUGHFARE

THROUGH THE

LINKS.

*Right:* A rare postcard
showing not just the
clubhouse but also a map
of the original course at
Aberystwyth.

*Below:* The clubhouse at
Aberystwyth, elegant and
atmospheric.

Golf Club Pavilion, Aberystwyth.

The clubhouse of Holyhead Golf Club.

mighty challenge when stormy winds from the Irish Sea batter and buffet the course. Then it looks and feels as if you are standing in the middle of a painting by J. M. W. Turner.

Local legend declares that the course came into existence when the Superintendent of the London & North Western Railway learned that the seaman on the company boats to Ireland usually spent their leisure time playing golf. He decided to try the game for himself and, soon besotted, persuaded the railway to build the course for guests at the Holyhead Hotel. The course and hotel prospered for several years until high-speed trains made them untenable, whereupon the members bought the course for £10,000 and proceeded to run it as a private enterprise.

Holyhead has hosted many quality tournaments over the years, including the Welsh Amateur Strokeplay and both the Welsh Girls' and Welsh Boys' Amateur Championships.

The course is quite undulating, but the real problems come with the steep moguls that litter several of the fairways. Heather and gorse proliferate and the views of the elevated tee on the tenth are stunning. At just over 6,000 yards, this is not a long course, but when the wind gets up, it certainly feels like you are preparing for a marathon.

## BULL BAY GOLF CLUB

Bull Bay Golf Club lies just outside the town of Amlwch on Anglesey and is the most northerly golf course in Wales. This is a heathland course, being set on land given to the club by the Marquess of Anglesey, who not only provided the land but paid for it to be built and also provided the original clubhouse.

Designed by Herbert Fowler in 1913, the course lies on a headland that is often swept by wind and rain. An exhibition match between James Braid and J. H. Taylor marked the opening of the course. This match was memorable because Braid took an eight at the third hole after failing to get his ball across a small ravine – and that, surely, gives hope to us all.

Bull Bay Golf Club in Anglesey.

David Lloyd George, British Prime Minister and devoted golfer, always regarded this as one of his favourite courses.

Thick gorse lines many of the fairways, although, despite the wind, there are also trees fringing several of the greens. Eleven of these greens are slightly elevated, while many of the fairways stretch out below the tee. This often tricks golfers into lashing at the ball, with the result that the thick rough on either side of the fairways claims another victim. Think accuracy and you won't go far wrong on this testing and demanding heathland layout.

## MILFORD HAVEN GOLF CLUB

Overlooking the magnificent Milford Haven waterway and founded in 1913, Milford Haven Golf Club is a fascinating Pembrokeshire course, one that happily takes its place alongside Tenby as one of the most difficult tracks of golf in this part of the country. Local historians will tell you that there are several early references to golf courses in the Pill and Marble Hall areas of the town prior to 1913, but no firm evidence exists regarding the history and dates of these first establishments.

What is known is that the site of the original Milford Haven Golf Club was in Goosepill, but in 1933, the club moved to its present location at Hubberston on the western edge of the town.

It is interesting to think that, when Milford Haven Golf Club first came into being in 1913, the Haven waterway was usually filled with warships of the Royal Navy. Over the last fifty years, it has been oil tankers – along with the massive oil refineries that still line the Haven side – that have dominated the waterway. With the coming of the oil refineries, there was an increase in the population of the area and many of these newcomers wished to play golf. Therefore, Milford Haven was extended to a full eighteen holes in 1978, the opening ceremony being performed by Welsh Ryder Cup player Brian Huggett. Several of the new holes take you out towards the Haven and the wind has now become a major factor in how you play them.

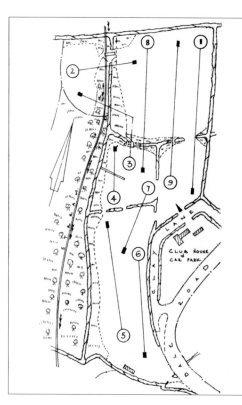

# MILFORD HAVEN GOLF CLUB

## LOCAL RULES

1  **Out of Bounds**—No. 9 hole—Ball lying to the right of the dividing hedge between 9 and 8, marked by red and white marker posts. Penalty stroke and distance.

2  Ball lying in drainage ditches may be lifted and dropped not nearer the hole. Penalty, one stroke.

| Strokes | Holes | Diff. in H'cap. | Single | 4 some |
|---|---|---|---|---|
| 1 | 6 | 1 | 1 | 0 |
| 2 | 6 15 | 2 | 2 | 1 |
| 3 | 6 9 15 | 3 | 2 | 1 |
| 4 | 6 9 15 18 | 4 | 3 | 2 |
| 5 | 1 6 9 15 18 | 5 | 4 | 2 |
| 6 | 1 6 9 10 15 18 | 6 | 5 | 3 |
| 7 | 1 5 6 9 10 15 18 | 7 | 5 | 3 |
| 8 | 1 5 6 9 10 14 15 18 | 8 | 6 | 3 |
| 9 | 1 3 5 6 9 10 14 15 18 | 9 | 7 | 3 |
| 10 | 1 3 5 6 9 10 12 14 15 18 | 10 | 8 | 4 |
| 11 | 1 3 5 6 8 9 10 12 14 15 18 | 11 | 8 | 4 |
| 12 | 1 3 5 6 8 9 10 12 14 15 17 18 | 12 | 9 | 5 |
| 13 | 1 3 4 5 6 8 9 10 12 14 15 17 18 | 13 | 10 | 5 |
| 14 | 1 3 4 5 6 8 9 10 12 13 14 15 17 18 | 14 | 11 | 5 |
| 15 | 1 2 3 4 5 6 8 9 10 12 13 14 15 17 18 | 15 | 11 | 6 |
| 16 | 1 2 3 4 5 6 8 9 10 11 12 13 14 15 17 18 | 16 | 12 | 6 |
| 17 | 1 2 3 4 5 6 7 8 9 10 11 12 13 14 15 17 18 | 17 | 13 | 6 |
| 18 | 1 2 3 4 5 6 7 8 9 10 11 12 13 14 15 16 17 18 | 18 | 14 | 7 |

*TABLE SHOWING WHERE STROKES ARE TAKEN.*

An early course map of Milford Haven Golf Club when it was still a nine-hole course.

The clubhouse at Milford Haven.

The present clubhouse is solid and imposing. It was once a private residence, known as Woodbine House. Bought by the club in 1965, it has somehow managed to retain the feel of a private house. The course is meadowland in style, but really it is the wind and weather conditions on this exposed part of the coast that determine how you are going to play – and the results of your efforts.

## DINAS POWIS GOLF CLUB

Straddling the flanks of a steep ridge to the west of Cardiff, Dinas Powis Golf Club came into existence on the very eve of the First World War. This was in 1914, although the creation of the club had been under discussion since 1912. Willie Park Jr from Musselborough was engaged to advise on the development, but in fact, Harry Prosser, the club's first professional/ groundsman, probably had far more to do with the eventual laying out of the course.

In the early days, there was great debate as to whether or not golf should be played here on a Sunday. After much discussion, the decision was reached – golf could be played, but there was to be no labour on that day. The club professional, it was stated, could please himself.

Being brought into creation in the very last days of peace, Dinas Powis Golf Club suffered the ignominy of having its fairways turned into potato fields shortly after play began – a hardship that had to be endured again during the Second World War. To begin with this was a nine-hole layout, but in 1921, with the help of James Braid, a second nine was created.

The short par three seventh, involving an almost vertical climb and a drive with a sand wedge, is one of the strangest holes you will ever encounter – strange but utterly compelling. On the other hand, the sixteenth, a downhill par four that bends around flanking bushes and trees on the left, was voted by Peter Alliss as one of his favourite holes of golf.

The eighteenth green and clubhouse of Dinas Powis.

Anglesey Golf Club at Rhosneigr.

Clubhouse at Rhosneigr.

## ANGLESEY GOLF CLUB

The Anglesey Golf Club lies at Rhosneigr, eight miles south of Holyhead. It is the oldest club on Anglesey and was created at the end of an era when sport had gradually become available for all. The club also benefited from the enormous growth of tourism in the years before the First World War and was brought into existence as a result of collaboration among local businessmen who suddenly saw something of a niche market. They rented several acres of common land and employed Harold Hilton, British Open and US Amateur Champion, to design and build a course.

Anglesey Golf Club opened in October 1914, two months after war had been declared against Germany, just in time to catch the last of the tourist trade before privations and rationing ended such luxury for the duration. Laid out on flat seaside terrain with tough patches of heather and several sand dunes, this was a typical links course with, from the beginning, a full eighteen holes.

During the Second World War, the RAF commandeered fourteen of these holes, but undaunted, the club simply purchased more land and created fourteen new holes – 'under the bridge' as members called them.

Anglesey Golf Club has always offered a warm welcome to visitors, either those on the way to Ireland or those intending to stop on the island. At 6,300 yards in length, it offers a good test of golf, and as you would expect in this part of the world, the wind has more than a little part to play here.

## LLANDUDNO (MAESDU) GOLF CLUB

The course at Maesdu lies virtually opposite the Llandudno (North Wales) Club but it is very different from its near neighbour. Whereas the North Wales Club is a true links, this is much more of a combined links and parkland layout.

Maesdu Golf Club was founded in 1915 when the First World War was at its height, one of only two clubs in Wales to open during the war years, and there was considerable opposition to the new club within the town. Fortunately, the local council decided that a second course in the area was needed in order to boost tourism – a quite amazing decision in view of the war that was currently raging in Europe – and permission was given to build Maesdu. It was the first municipally owned golf course in Wales. The design of the course has changed several times, although the present layout has been played for at least forty years.

The club's first professional, Tom Jones, along with James Braid, laid out the course. Jones stayed in charge for over fifty years and later, in 1962, went on to become captain of the club. Maesdu has always been a good test of golf and has hosted many important events over

The course at Maesdu, Llandudno.

the years. These included the Penfold Tournament in the 1950s and 1960s when players like Henry Cotton and Peter Alliss graced the fairways.

The course undulates gently up and down the slopes, making it relatively easy walking. The wind can obviously play a part here, and the ditches and rough provide even more of a problem. The views off the course are inspiring, whether they be inland towards the hills or out towards the Irish Sea.

Llandudno (Maesdu) became a members' course in 1974, and in 1995, the council granted the club a ninety-nine-year lease. Llandudno is surely lucky to have two great courses like Maesdu and the North Wales Club.

Whitchurch Golf Club, always one of the best-maintained courses in Wales.

## WHITCHURCH GOLF CLUB

Whitchurch Golf Club is one of the most beautifully maintained and manicured courses in Wales. It has hosted many important championship events and the condition of its fairways and greens often beguiles visitors into not giving the course the respect it so richly deserves. A round of golf at Whitchurch is a testing and memorable experience – but a hugely enjoyable one, too.

The course was founded in 1915, during the First World War, although planning for its inception had been going on for some time. Originally, it was intended to provide nothing more than a little sport to the well-off people of Cardiff who were not able to gain entry into other clubs in the area. As such, it simply provided a few holes for people to knock a ball around. However, the popularity of the course and the environment soon grew to such an extent that James Braid and Frank Johns were called in to design a proper course. The present layout remains much the same as the gem that they created.

The course meanders its way through the tall trees and thick bushes that litter this parkland stretch of ground. There is an air of peace and calm at Whitchurch, despite being located close to the M4 and alongside the A470, one of the main roads into Cardiff. At just over 6,000 yards, there are great chances for birdies here, but stray off line and you will be severely punished.

Whitchurch has produced many fine golfers over the years, none better than Walker Cup player and captain Nigel Edwards. In 2008, Whitchurch was also voted the Best Inland Course in Wales by the Welsh Club Golfer.

# THE YEARS OF DEPRESSION
## 1920 TO 1945

The end of the Great War should have meant a return to normal – or even to a better world. That was why people had fought the war, why they had endured over four years of hell in the mud of Flanders and the heat of the Middle East. In reality, however, the world that men and women returned to was, in some cases, exactly the same and sometimes very much worse.

By 1919, Britain was virtually bankrupt, and as the 1920s unfolded, it soon became apparent that a global Depression was about to hit. If golf clubs thought that they had endured the worst and that happy times were ahead, they were very much mistaken. Unemployment soared, the middle classes being hit almost as hard as the working men or women.

Sport, leisure and recreation were the last things on people's minds. Earning a living, surviving hardships and depravation, was much more important.

The glory days of the early 1900s may have gone, but there were still a handful of golf clubs created in the 1920s through to the outbreak of the Second World War in 1939. Many of these have survived until the present day, although some like the Leys just outside St Athan and Aberthaw have long since disappeared.


## CLYNE GOLF CLUB

Clyne Golf Club is situated on Clyne Common, 600 feet above Swansea and the Mumbles with, on the one hand, magnificent views out over the Bristol Channel and, behind, the Brecon Beacons and Black Mountains. The club was founded in 1920 and registered as a limited company. Although defined as a links, it is really a moorland layout. The course sits almost at the entrance to the Gower Peninsula, bordering Fairwood Park Golf Club, and just a few miles away from Pennard.

Messrs Colt and Harries, the same renowned team of architects who designed Pyle & Kenfig Golf Club, created the Clyne course. Virtually none of the holes have been changed, although the turf has altered in character over the years as a result of the fertilisation. The ground is undulating and offers the golfer numerous natural hazards as well as a large number of bunkers. Gorse and bracken are to be found on many of the holes, but because of its position high upon the downs, there are almost no trees on the course.

The course at Clyne is set out in two distinct loops of nine, making what is virtually a figure-of-eight shape. The first, tenth, ninth and eighteenth greens are therefore conveniently situated close to the clubhouse.

At just over 6,000 yards, Clyne has a par of 70 and a stroke index of 68. This makes it a great test of golf and one of the finest courses on Gower – one not to be missed.


## BRYNHILL GOLF CLUB

Brynhill Golf Club began life with a meeting at Barry YMCA in 1921 when an agreement was reached to pay the tenant farmer who owned land on the northern edge of Barry the sum of £3 per annum in order to create a new golf club. The farmer was also allowed to graze his

*Above:* The Welsh Ladies' International side for the Home International Matches, 1922.

*Left:* Golf in the 1920s.

The clubhouse at Clyne.

A breathtaking view from the Clyne fairways across to the Mumbles.

The eighteenth green and clubhouse at Brynhill.

sheep across the course. Professional golfer Ted Ray was brought in to pick out the tees and greens but members did much of the construction work themselves.

The club was officially opened on 28 May 1921, the original clubhouse being a portable shed borrowed from nearby Barry Docks. The first club professional was Mr D. J. Rees, father of famous Ryder Cup player and captain Dai Rees, who was himself a member of Brynhill.

Interestingly, the opening or inaugural match on the course was filmed by the manager of Barry's Theatre Royal, being shown at the cinema that night, surely one of the first times that golf had ever appeared on the silver screen.

To begin with, Brynhill consisted of just nine holes. Even so, with the demands of the war effort being the main concern, during the Second World War, some of the land was used to house American GIs. In 1948, the club bought more land and new holes were designed. In October 1984, a brand-new clubhouse was opened, the American film star and comedian Bob Hope (who had family in the area) performing the opening ceremony.

The final stages of golf-course development were completed in 1998 when an extra 65 acres were brought into play. Brynhill now offers a great test of parkland golf.

## ABERDARE GOLF CLUB

Aberdare Golf Club sits at the top end of the Cynon Valley, surrounded by hills and mature woodlands. Founded in 1921 by local businessmen from the town of Aberdare, the course is a fascinating mixture of parkland and mountainside. The fairways tend to run across the hillsides rather than directly up and down them, so that, although there are steep slopes on the course, it is still relatively easy walking.

There are a number of blind holes here, but one of the most fascinating is the second. The green sits down at the bottom of a slope alongside the clubhouse and you cannot see it until you are virtually on top of it. The hole is intriguing, one of many quirky little designs you will find on this excellent Valley course.

*Right:* Driving off the third at Aberdare, the old clubhouse in the background.

*Below:* The original clubhouse at Pyle & Kenfig Golf Club, which burnt down in the 1920s.

Aberdare Golf Club was where Ryder Cup captain Dai Rees moulded and honed his game. His father, D. J. Rees, was the club professional for many years and the great Dai often strode these fairways in his early playing days.

Aberdare Golf Club was, for many years, home to the Golden Lamp competition, a prestigious amateur trophy won, amongst others, by people like Bargoed golfer David Price – now, with his wife Kathryn, one of the club professionals.

Aberdare is one of the gems of Welsh golf, always well maintained and designed to both test and reward quality play.

## PYLE & KENFIG GOLF CLUB

Pyle & Kenfig Golf Club was created when the golfers of Newton Nottage Golf Club (founded in 1919) decided to move from the area that is now known as Sandy Bay Caravan Park. It is not clear why the decision was made, but in 1921, negotiations began with the Trustees of the Borough of Kenfig in order to create a new golf course on Waun-y-Mer Common, and the following year, Pyle & Kenfig Golf Club was up and running.

Designed by Harry Colt, P&K (as the course is always affectionately known) is literally a course of two halves. The first nine is pure downland, with a proliferation of gorse and bracken, and being wide open to the elements. The nature of the grass and the location of the greens force you to play approach shots like a links, something that will stand you in good stead for what you are about to experience. The second nine is pure, unadulterated links golf: huge sand dunes and thick tufted grass making this one of the most difficult stretches of golf in South Wales.

Widening of the cart track that used to bisect the fairways and commandeering of land by the Army during the Second World War caused some redesigning of the course. Mackenzie Ross was brought in to carry out this work, redesigning holes eleven to fifteen – he described the area as 'a veritable golfer's paradise'.

The wind is always a crucial factor at P&K, particularly on the short par threes, which have to be played well, as, invariably, they prove to be the make or break of any round. P&K has hosted many top-quality events, including the Men's Home International matches, and was a qualifying venue for the 1998 British Amateur Championships. Along with Royal Porthcawl and Southerndown, it is considered to be one of the top links courses in South East Wales.

Henry Cotton holds a golf clinic at Pyle & Kenfig Golf Club.

One of the original nine holes at Newport, Pembs.

## NEWPORT LINKS (PEMBROKESHIRE)

Of all the golf courses in Wales, Newport Links – Newport (Pembs) as it was originally known – has to be one of the most atmospheric and enjoyable. Anyone who has played it will readily acknowledge that it is another of Wales' hidden gems. Founded in 1925, this beautiful seaside links was, for many years, a nine-hole course, one of the few nine-hole links in the country. In the early years of the twenty-first century, the course was extended to a full eighteen holes, the original nine now providing the back portion of the course.

The course is set on the Nevern Estuary in the Pembrokeshire Coastal National Park and is overlooked by Carningli Mountain (the Mountain of the Angels). It offers glorious views out to sea and, over the estuary, towards the ancient Norman settlement and castle of Newport.

There are some glorious holes here, notably the fourteenth and the wonderful par three fifteenth where you really have no option other than to hit the green with your drive. The new holes sit on sloping land behind the clubhouse and have already proved beneficial to the club. Such is the quality of the new layout, it has already attracted attention as a championship venue and, in 2009, hosted the South Wales Boys' Championship.

Newport Links has an excellent clubhouse, but in addition, there is also high-quality accommodation available. You can stay on the course, eat in the clubhouse, and play this magnificent North Pembrokeshire links whenever you like – golf at its very best.

## LLANWERN GOLF CLUB

Situated just to the east of Newport, Llanwern Golf Club is one of the oldest clubs in East Wales. Founded in 1928 by three local businessmen, it is also one of the most popular. Much of the original course is now covered by a housing estate, and the present layout lies in the shadow of the old steel works. That does not detract in any way from the scenic nature of this attractive and atmospheric course.

Percy Alliss and Henry Cotton playing at Llanwern Golf Club in 1928.

Originally a nine-hole course, Llanwern was extended to a full eighteen in 1937, the occasion being marked by an exhibition match involving Walter Hagen and Joe Kirkwood. Much of the early popularity of Llanwern was due to the close proximity of the railway station, just 200 yards from the clubhouse. Unfortunately, this was closed in the Beeching cuts of the 1960s.

Llanwern has not lost all its connection with the railway, however, as two of its fairways run parallel with the Cardiff to London railway line. It is not unusual to see busy commuters staring out through the carriage windows, desperately wishing that they could be out on the course rather than heading for a day in the office.

The course is relatively flat, apart from one or two steep climbs. However, it is the tree-lined fairways and thick rough/bushes that cause most problems. You really do need to hit long and straight on this course, and a good card can be totally wrecked on the club's own 'Amen Corner' – the eighth, ninth, and tenth holes.

At 6,200 yards in length, most of Llanwern's fairways slope from north to south. The greens are tricky to read and you will really need all of your game in order to take on this lovely parkland course.

## BUILTH WELLS GOLF CLUB
Before 1922, anybody from the Builth Wells area who wished to play golf had to make a journey of nearly seven miles to Llangammarch Wells. Then a group of local businessmen purchased the Park Farm, selling off part of it in order to fund the project and building a nine-hole course on the 49 acres that remained. The sixteenth-century Welsh long house that had previously housed the farmer was converted into a clubhouse. Still in use, in 2004, this old farmhouse was extended, and it is more than likely that this Grade II listed building is the oldest golf clubhouse in the country.

*Right and below:* The old and the new (well, newer) clubhouse at Builth Wells.

The early years of Builth Wells Golf Club were a struggle, the original members having to work on the course as well as playing their games. The local brewer offered his dray horses to pull the mowers along the fairways, the horses wearing specially made shoes so as not to damage the turf.

During the Second World War, much of the course was ploughed up, although parts of it were still playable for members and visitors – in particular, the American GIs who were stationed in the area. After the war, the course was increased in length, but by the 1970s, it was obvious that another nine holes were needed. This did not happen until 1985 when Builth Wells finally became a members' club.

The course remains very picturesque and is always well maintained. There is no par five on the course, but it still takes great skill to play this one anywhere close to your handicap.

A group of original members at Builth Wells.

Miss Mary Jeffries plays the first shot at Glynneath Golf Club, August 1932.

Glynneath's clubhouse before a new extension was added.

## GLYNNEATH GOLF CLUB

At a meeting in the office of the local paper, *The Star,* on 5 May 1931, a group of like-minded people gathered together to discuss the possibility of creating a local golf club. In true democratic fashion, a committee was appointed to investigate the possibility of such a venture. Before long, land was leased from the owners of Penycraig Farm and a course had been laid out by members. Glynneath Golf Club had begun its life.

The terrain on which the course was set was difficult, and tees had to be created on such small flat areas as were available, while the greens were created on level land that had been cut out of the hillside – amazingly, many of these original putting surfaces are still in play. The official opening of the club came on 25 August 1932 when Mrs Mary Jeffries drove the first ball.

The original clubhouse was a corrugated-iron building, the bar being a small room containing a barrel of beer brought up from the village of Glynneath with a stable door being used as a hatch. The only heating was a 'tortoise stove' in the centre of the room. Such were the social arrangements for many years until a new clubhouse was finally opened in 1978. That same year, work began on lengthening the course to a full eighteen holes.

Glynneath is a parkland layout with one or two steep climbs. Water comes into play on several of the holes and the sloping fairways mean that you have to be accurate as well as long with your drives. Tall trees sometimes encroach from the side of the fairways, making this a course to manage your way around rather than one where you can just stand up and hit the skin off the ball.

# THE POSTWAR YEARS
# 1945 TO PRESENT

As you would expect, there were no new golf courses founded during the Second World War, 1939 to 1945. Indeed, many courses – if not most of them – lost their fairways on a temporary basis as the government commandeered nearly all available land in order to grow crops for the war effort. Despite this, golf, albeit of a restricted kind, continued to be played. And sometimes it was a dangerous pastime.

At Pontypridd Golf Club in 1941, a German Junkers 88 appeared over the course, causing players to dive for cover in the thick rough. Nobody was sure if the plane opened fire, but those on the course certainly swore that it did! Some clubs even introduced local rules to say that a player whose stroke was affected by a bomb or shell explosion could play another ball from the same spot – with a one-stroke penalty, naturally.

While the Welsh clubs invariably recovered their land once hostilities were over, it took many years to bring them up to the standard at which they were really playable again. It was very much a labour of love.

The immediate postwar period saw a gradual re-emergence of interest in golf as players returned home from foreign climes and picked up their clubs once more. However, no new courses were founded in Wales until 1962, when the St Pierre course opened at Chepstow. It was a slow beginning. By contrast, from 1970 onwards, there was an incredible growth of new clubs, no fewer than seventy-two new courses being created in Wales between then and the end of the century.

Most of these new courses came into existence in the 1990s, many of them being proprietary establishments rather than member-owned clubs, as farmers realised there was undoubtedly more money to be made out of providing leisure facilities than in working with milk quotas and the like. For the golfer, however, what this sudden increase in clubs meant was that there were no longer things like club waiting lists and more people have now been able to play the game than ever before. Golf has at last truly become a people's sport.

New courses in this period have included INCO (now known as Tawe Vale) in 1965, Cradoc (1967), Bryn Meadows (1974), Greenmeadow (1979), Dewstow (1988), Alice Springs (1989), Woodlake Park (1993), Trefloyne (1996), and of course, Celtic Manor (1995).

## MARRIOTT ST PIERRE GOLF CLUB

The history of the estate and house at St Pierre goes back over a thousand years, but golf on these rolling and picturesque meadows is a relatively recent development. It dates from 1962, when Bill Graham bought the estate and created a high-quality golf course – the Old Course, as it is now known – and sporting complex that quickly made its mark.

The original house or mansion was opened as a club in 1961, and with Ken Cotton appointed as course architect, the original course was soon designed and laid out. Unbelievably, it was open for play within twelve months. In the opinion of many, this is still the finest course design or layout in Wales. And from the beginning, St Pierre began to attract the attention of tournament organisers. Clearly, this was not just any old golf course.

The Welsh International team visiting Glynneath in 1964, Huw Phillips and Iestyn Tucker on the second tee.

A ladies' match at Porthcawl.

The original mansion house at St Pierre.

One of the wonderfully scenic holes at St Pierre.

The first important tournament held at St Pierre was the Welsh Open. It was followed in 1971 by the Dunlop Masters, and then by the Silk Cut Masters – Welshman Ian Woosnam winning his first important professional event in this tournament in 1983. The Epson Matchplay and Strokeplay tournaments were also held at St Pierre until 1991, while the Curtis Cup and the Solheim Cup have both been contested over the fairways.

Huge oak and chestnut trees, some of them dating back 500 years, provide and interesting challenge on the Old Course. The par three final hole, across a wide lake, has to be the gem of the course. St Pierre also has another course, the Mathern, and the complex also offers other sports, including squash, tennis, and badminton. Now owned by the Marriott Group, the accommodation at St Pierre is first class.

## BRYN MEADOWS GOLF CLUB

Bryn Meadows is inevitably linked to the dynamic personality of Brian Mayo, the founder and moving force behind the complex. Along with two business associates, Mayo purchased the land at Hengoed in Mid Glamorgan, and by 1974, the course was up and running.

In 1979, a freak accident, after Mayo licked a golf ball that had been contaminated by weed-killer, resulted in him eventually losing both his legs. The tragedy would have killed many lesser men – not Brian Mayo. Determined not to let it ruin his life, Mayo amazingly bought out his two partners, battled his way back to fitness and created a golfing complex that soon earned a national reputation for quality and friendliness.

Although Brian passed away in January 1999, his two sons now run the golf complex at Bryn Meadows as a family concern. As well as a quality golf course, it boasts a superb state-of-the-art leisure suite and a first-class hotel.

The fairways at Bryn Meadows are tight and tree-lined, offering a different test on every hole. The club claims two signature holes. The par five second takes you down the edge of the course with out-of-bounds on the right and a third shot that will bring you over a wide pond. Water also comes into play on the second signature hole, the par three thirteenth that has a 227-yard carry over a wide lake.

Springtime at
Bryn Meadows.

Brian Mayo always said that his inspiration to overcome such a crippling accident came from Douglas Bader's story, as told in the book and film *Reach for the Sky*. As a consequence, he founded the British Amputee Golf Open, raising thousands of pounds for amputee charities. For many years, the event was played at Bryn Meadows, a fitting tribute to an amazing character.

## CRADOC GOLF CLUB

Cradoc Golf Club owes its origins to the Penoyre Golf & Country Club. This was an attempt by a small number of golfers, originally from Brecon Golf Club, to form a club on the Penoyre Estate just outside Brecon. Designed by Ken Cotton, the eighty-year-old course architect arrived on site at eleven, mapped out seventeen holes by lunch and finished his job by teatime.

The course was opened in May 1969, the land being leased from Penoyre. Members, however, wanted a sounder footing and therefore negotiations with the estate at Penoyre continued for some years. During this period, the clubhouse, which had been located in the old mansion house, was lost, and for a while, it seemed that the same thing might happen to the course itself. It was a financially turbulent period, when members had to put in huge amounts of time and effort to fundraise and work on the course. However, in March 1978, everything finally came to fulfilment. The course was saved and a brand-new clubhouse was built. Cradoc Golf Club had come into being.

Cradoc is now the largest golf club in mid-Wales. It is a parkland course with wonderful views of the Brecon Beacons. The views off the top of the course are nothing short of

Stunning views of the Brecon Beacons off the course at Cradoc.

The Brecon Beacons in their winter garb.

spectacular, although some of the steeper climbs – which gave access to even better views – have recently been taken out and several holes redesigned.

Cradoc is a testing but rewarding golf course, one that displays maturity beyond its years. With great practice facilities and a good clubhouse, this is an ideal society venue and one that will intrigue anybody who loves the game of golf.

## THE VALE RESORT

The Vale golf resort lies in beautiful parkland, the fairways winding their way through woods, around lakes and across streams. These days, there are two championship courses available at the Vale: the Lake and the Wales National. Although the complex has only been open since 1991, both courses have already hosted important championship events.

The Vale began life as a 27-hole layout. These were the full Lake course and a small nine-hole course known as Hensol. This latter course has now been incorporated into the Wales National course.

The two courses currently available are very different in character. The Lake, interestingly enough, relies on sloping fairways – no such thing as a level lie on some of these holes – and mature trees for its protection. Water does play a significant part in the course layout, particularly on the ninth and eighteenth, while the par four twelfth offers an island green that requires skill and courage if you are going to come away with a par or even a bogey.

The Wales National retains an almost 'American' feel to it – big greens with lots of borrows and slopes, and plenty of water just waiting to catch a miss-hit ball. Many of the fairways are quite narrow and require the golfer to plot his or her way around. Use of a

Plenty of water on the Vale's National course.

Beware the water in front of the green on this downhill par four at the Vale.

driver on this course is not always recommended, unless you are very accurate. Some of the walks to the next tee when you come off the greens are a little on the long side and the use of a buggy is recommended.

The hotel at the Vale is luxurious and well appointed with views out over the Lake course. The golf clubhouse is a separate entity from the hotel but is equally as comfortable.

## NORTHOP COUNTRY PARK GOLF CLUB

Designed by Ryder Cup player and world-recognised golf teacher John Jacobs, Northop Park was established in 1993. It has now developed into one of the finest inland golfing venues in the country. The course has already hosted the Welsh Professional Championships, the British Girls' Championship and the Girls' Home Internationals. In the years ahead, it will undoubtedly be the venue for many more important events.

Set in a tranquil parkland environment, one of the features of the course is the proliferation of tall and mature trees. This is an easy-walking, flat course, but it is one that provides a stiff challenge for golfers of all abilities. Improved drainage and continual developmental work on the course ensures that Northop is playable all year round and offers good value to visitors.

Recent work on the par five eleventh has produced what is now the longest hole in Wales – 617 yards in length. The sixteenth, a dog-legged par four, is one of the best holes on the course. Water lurks out on the right, tall trees guard the left, and a stream runs across the fairway in front of the green.

The complex at Northop offers a Georgian-style clubhouse, tennis courts, sauna and gymnasium. There is also a driving range. Easily reached, just off the A55 Expressway, Northop Park lies 3 miles to the south of Flint. It is an essential stop for anyone who wishes to experience championship golf in North Wales.

Just one of Northop's stunningly beautiful holes.

The clubhouse at Northop.

## THE CELTIC MANOR RESORT

The golfing vision to bring the Ryder Cup to Wales in 2010 began back in 1993, when legendary golf course architect Robert Trent Jones was persuaded to create his first golf course in the land of his fathers by Celtic Manor owner, Sir Terry Matthews.

Named the Roman Road, after the ancient Via Julia, which once crossed the site, the course opened in July 1995 along with a vast timber-framed clubhouse, which also housed a gymnasium, swimming pool, spa, and conference rooms. By the following year, an eighteen-hole academy course, Coldra Woods, had also been constructed to another Trent Jones design and was unveiled alongside a state-of-the-art golf academy.

With ambitions to host major tournaments taking shape, Robert Trent Jones Jr was commissioned to build a spectacular new championship course, the Wentwood Hills, which was officially launched by Ryder Cup captains present and future, Mark James and Ian Woosnam, in 1999, the same year Celtic Manor opened its sumptuous 330-bedroom resort hotel and convention centre.

Wentwood Hills staged the Celtic Manor Wales Open on the European Tour from 2000-2004, but while the resort and Wales were bidding for the Ryder Cup in 2001, its steep slopes were deemed unsuitable for moving the vast numbers of spectators around safely. Undeterred, Sir Terry Matthews took one more bold and ambitious step by promising to build nine brand-new holes on land newly acquired adjacent to the flatter holes of Wentwood Hills and create the Twenty Ten Course.

Ross McMurray of European Golf Design has used the hillside, which was such a disadvantage to the now-defunct Wentwood Hills layout, to provide fantastic viewing banks over the closing four holes that also look out over many of the earlier holes in the floor of the Usk Valley below. As you might expect from a course purpose-built for the Ryder Cup, plenty of match-play drama has also been thrown in, particularly on the back nine of the Twenty Ten Course, which measures 7,493 yards and plays to a par of 71.

Water, rough and trees come into play at the Celtic Manor's new Ryder Cup course.

Many of the discarded holes from the old championship course, along with two new par threes, have now been remodelled by Colin Montgomerie to include signature pot bunkers and form the front nine of a course that bears his name, the Montgomerie. Opening just after the Twenty Ten Course in July 2007, the back nine of this 6,351-yard, par 69 course has been built on land that formerly housed the Coldra Woods academy course.

With the original Roman Road Course (6,515 yards, par 70) still standing, Celtic Manor now boasts three championship courses. With its golf academy upgraded to become the Wales National Centre of Excellence, the resort can lay claim to being one of the most complete golfing complexes in Europe.

## COTTRELL PARK GOLF CLUB

Founded in 1996, Cottrell Park Golf Club sits just off A48 at St Nicholas between Cardiff and Cowbridge. The club boasts two testing and demanding courses: the Mackintosh and the Button Gwinnett. There is also a driving range and excellent clubhouse facilities. Set in rolling parkland, the courses are laid out on historic land that at various times has belonged to the Mackintosh, Button and Gwinnett families and has a history that dates back to the medieval period. The estate was eventually purchased by William Powell & Sons and, in the days before the arrival of the golf courses, was used for agricultural purposes.

The original courses were the Mackintosh and a small nine-hole course called the Button. Both were founded in 1996. The Button has since been extended and developed into a full eighteen-hole championship course now known as the Button Gwinnett.

*Left:* One of the testing holes on the Montgomerie course at the Celtic Manor.

*Below:* The Roman Road course at the Celtic Manor.

Golfers putt out on one of Cottrell Park's testing holes.

Expect beautiful views on both of Cottrell Park's courses.

*Left:* The signature hole at Machynys.

*Below:* The wood-lined and atmospheric clubhouse at Machynys.

The Mackintosh has developed into a mature and testing parkland course that offers the opportunity to stand up and open your shoulders on some holes. At other times, however, a shorter drive will give you greater accuracy to the green. The course has already hosted several championship events.

The Button Gwinnett is again a parkland layout with tall trees, water and, over the last few holes in particular, steep climbs offering serious challenges for the golfer. Sweeping panoramic views take in the Brecon Beacons to the north and the Bristol Channel to the south. Keep your mind on the game, however, as this course – and the Mackintosh – will undoubtedly test all areas of your game. Due to its higher position, some of the holes on the Button Gwinnett play more like a mountaintop course than a parkland one, especially in the hot summer months.

Cottrell Park is easily reached from Cardiff and Newport and is the ideal venue for people who would like a full day of golf.

## MACHYNYS PENINSULA GOLF AND COUNTRY CLUB

Opened in April 2005, Machynys Golf Club sits on the edge of the estuary with magnificent views out over Carmarthen Bay and the north Gower Peninsula. The course is just 20 minutes from the M4, on the outskirts of Llanelli, and is Wales' most recent links-style development.

However, this is very much a modern links with plenty of internal water – the external does not really come into play. The wind, naturally enough, is an ever-present factor on this tough and demanding – but ultimately rewarding – championship course.

Designed by the Nicklaus design company, the project being overseen by Jack's son Gary, there are many spectacular holes here. The fourth and fifth are both interesting but it is on the sixteenth, where you drive over a wide lake, that the course really comes into its own. The eighteenth is a spectacular finishing hole, again taking you across water onto a fairway that snakes back towards the clubhouse. The last few holes are real card-wreckers unless you take great care and play them with more than a degree of caution.

The clubhouse at Machynys is wood-lined and atmospheric, the food being of an exceptional standard. A wide veranda or balcony runs around two sides of the building, the ideal place to sit with a drink in your hand, watching players contending with the huge bunker that runs across the fairway in front of the final green.

Machynys has recently opened a new driving range and teaching academy, the ideal place to hone your game before taking on the challenges of the course itself. If you feel like indulging yourself, there is also a health spa, a sauna, and a gymnasium – or else, you can just sit in the bar and enjoy the atmosphere. The choice is yours.

# CONCLUSION

The history of golf in Wales may not be long, but it is certainly full and fascinating. There are many great clubs, all offering quality golf and an experience that you will find hard to better. The welcome, both on the course and in the clubhouses, is invariably second to none. Anybody who professes to enjoy the game of golf cannot fail to enjoy the experience of playing in Wales.

The coming of the Ryder Cup in 2010 is, to all intents and purposes, a seal on the quality of Welsh golf. Hopefully, visitors will come from all parts of the world to witness Europe and the USA in their biannual battle. More importantly, however, it is to be hoped that those same visitors will stay on to play and experience at least some of the Welsh golf courses.

Without wishing to detract from the quality of those courses along the M4 corridor – and some of the new golf complexes like Celtic Manor, the Vale and Machynys undoubtedly have to be played – no visitor could ever say that he has really experienced Welsh golf until he has strayed off the accepted route and tried those courses that lie not too far beyond the main trail across South Wales. Places like Builth Wells, Morlais Castle, Clyne, St David's, Newport Links and Aberystwyth are truly 'hidden gems' that have to be seen to be believed.

In the north of the country, there are magnificent courses like Nefyn – surely the most photographed course in Britain – Dolgellau and Bull Bay. These and many more are just waiting for the discerning visitor. And once played, they will quickly become unforgettable.

Finally, we feel it is essential to reiterate that the courses described and shown in this book are not the only tracks in Wales. There are so many more. But these, the ones described here, are favourites that have held places of affection in our hearts for many years. If you, too, be you visitor to the country or a resident, enjoy them as we have done, then the purpose of this book will be fulfilled.

*Above left:* Brian Huggett, Ryder Cup player and captain, seen here in action.

*Above right:* Lloyd George may not have been the most naturally talented golfer Wales has ever produced, but he was certainly one of the keenest.